UK 2024 Ninja Foo FlexDrawer Air Fryer Cookbook for Beginners

1500 Days of Delicious, Healthy & Energy-Saving Air Fryer Recipes for Complete Meals using Ninja Foodi FlexDrawer Air Fryer

Mai B. Wilkens

All Rights Reserved.

The contents of this book may not be reproduced, copied or transmitted without the direct written permission of the author or publisher. Under no circumstances will the publisher or the author be held responsible or liable for any damage, compensation or pecuniary loss arising directly or indirectly from the information contained in this book.

Legal notice. This book is protected by copyright. It is intended for personal use only. You may not modify, distribute, sell, use, quote or paraphrase any part or content of this book without the consent of the author or publisher.

Notice Of Disclaimer.

Please note that the information in this document is intended for educational and entertainment purposes only. Every effort has been made to provide accurate, up-to-date, reliable and complete information. No warranty of any kind is declared or implied. The reader acknowledges that the author does not engage in the provision of legal, financial, medical or professional advice. The content in this book has been obtained from a variety of sources. Please consult a licensed professional before attempting any of the techniques described in this book. By reading this document, the reader agrees that in no event shall the author be liable for any direct or indirect damages, including but not limited to errors, omissions or inaccuracies, resulting from the use of the information in this document.

CONTENTS

MEASUREMENT CONVERSIONS 10

Breakfast Recipes 12

French Toasts 12

Bacon, Cheese, And Avocado Melt & Cheesy Scrambled Eggs 12

Easy Sausage Pizza 12

Sausage And Egg Breakfast Burrito 13

Roasted Oranges 13

Savory Soufflé 13

Glazed Apple Fritters Glazed Peach Fritters 14

Mushroom-and-tomato Stuffed Hash Browns 14

Cinnamon Toast 15

Potatoes Lyonnaise 15

Breakfast Casserole 15

Bagels 16

Sausage With Eggs 16

Sweet Potatoes Hash 16

Banana And Raisins Muffins 17

Puff Pastry 17

Sausage And Cheese Balls 17

Banana Bread 18

Cinnamon-raisin Bagels Everything Bagels 18

Sausage Hash And Baked Eggs 19

Egg With Baby Spinach 19

Egg In Bread Hole 20

Blueberry Coffee Cake And Maple Sausage Patties 20

Buttermilk Biscuits With Roasted Stone Fruit Compote 21

Simple Bagels 21

Breakfast Bacon 22

Cauliflower Avocado Toast And All-in-one Toast 22

Parmesan Sausage Egg Muffins 23

Cheesy Baked Eggs 23

Parmesan Ranch Risotto And Oat And Chia Porridge 23

Strawberry Baked Oats Chocolate Peanut Butter Baked Oats 24

Breakfast Potatoes 24

Easy Pancake Doughnuts 25
Spinach Omelet And Bacon, Egg, And Cheese Roll Ups 25
Breakfast Pitta 25
French Toast Sticks 26
Canadian Bacon Muffin Sandwiches And All-in-one Toast 26
Perfect Cinnamon Toast 27
Cheddar-ham-corn Muffins 27
Breakfast Stuffed Peppers 27
Breakfast Cheese Sandwich 28
Donuts 28

Snacks And Appetizers Recipes 28
Fried Halloumi Cheese 28
Mozzarella Arancini 29
Sweet Bites 29
Goat Cheese And Garlic Crostini & Sweet Bacon Potato Crunchies 29
Ravioli 30
Onion Rings 30
Beef Taquitos 30
Potato Tater Tots 31
Kale Chips 31
Spicy Chicken Tenders 31
Miso-glazed Shishito Peppers Charred Lemon Shishito Peppers 32
Beef Jerky Pineapple Jerky 32
Lemony Pear Chips 33
Mozzarella Balls 33
Crispy Calamari Rings 33
Sausage Balls With Cheese 34
Chicken Tenders 34
Beef Skewers 34
Cinnamon Sugar Chickpeas 35
Crab Cakes 35
Crispy Tortilla Chips 35
Cottage Fries 36

Vegetables And Sides Recipes 36
Balsamic-glazed Tofu With Roasted Butternut Squash 36
Fried Avocado Tacos 37
Garlic-rosemary Brussels Sprouts 37

Mixed Air Fry Veggies 37
Sweet Potatoes & Brussels Sprouts 38
Zucchini With Stuffing 38
Potatoes & Beans 38
Buffalo Seitan With Crispy Zucchini Noodles 39
Breaded Summer Squash 39
Quinoa Patties 40
Garlic Herbed Baked Potatoes 40
Fried Artichoke Hearts 41
Balsamic Vegetables 41
Bacon Potato Patties 41
Beets With Orange Gremolata And Goat's Cheese 42
Garlic Potato Wedges In Air Fryer 42
Delicious Potatoes & Carrots 42
Jerk Tofu With Roasted Cabbage 43
Mushroom Roll-ups 43
Chickpea Fritters 44

Beef, Pork, And Lamb Recipes 44
Pork Chops With Brussels Sprouts 44
Sausage-stuffed Peppers 45
New York Strip Steak 45
Glazed Steak Recipe 45
Sausage And Cauliflower Arancini 46
Bacon-wrapped Vegetable Kebabs 46
Sausage Meatballs 46
Stuffed Beef Fillet With Feta Cheese 47
Filet Mignon Wrapped In Bacon 47
Steak Fajitas With Onions And Peppers 47
Beef Cheeseburgers 48
Kielbasa Sausage With Pineapple And Kheema Meatloaf 48
Seasoned Flank Steak 49
Simple Strip Steak 49
Pork Chops With Broccoli 49
Steak Bites With Cowboy Butter 50
Mojito Lamb Chops 50
Sumptuous Pizza Tortilla Rolls 50
Tomahawk Steak 51

Roast Souvlaki-style Pork With Lemon-feta Baby Potatoes ... 51
Lamb Shank With Mushroom Sauce ... 52
Korean Bbq Beef ... 52
Pigs In A Blanket With Spinach-artichoke Stuffed Mushrooms ... 53
Steak And Asparagus Bundles ... 53
Tasty Lamb Patties ... 54
Mozzarella Stuffed Beef And Pork Meatballs ... 54
Air Fryer Chicken-fried Steak ... 54
Garlic-rosemary Pork Loin With Scalloped Potatoes And Cauliflower ... 55
Pork Chops And Potatoes ... 55
Panko Crusted Calf's Liver Strips ... 56
Yogurt Lamb Chops ... 56
Beef Kofta Kebab ... 56

Fish And Seafood Recipes ... 57

Seasoned Tuna Steaks ... 57
Bacon-wrapped Shrimp ... 57
Air Fryer Calamari ... 57
Shrimp Po'boys With Sweet Potato Fries ... 58
Crusted Tilapia ... 58
Fish Tacos ... 59
Tuna-stuffed Quinoa Patties ... 59
Blackened Mahimahi With Honey-roasted Carrots ... 60
Steamed Cod With Garlic And Swiss Chard ... 60
Parmesan Mackerel With Coriander And Garlic Butter Prawns Scampi ... 61
Salmon Fritters With Courgette & Cajun And Lemon Pepper Cod ... 61
Shrimp With Lemon And Pepper ... 62
Healthy Lobster Cakes ... 62
Savory Salmon Fillets ... 62
Thai Prawn Skewers And Lemon-tarragon Fish En Papillote ... 63
Lemon-pepper Trout ... 63
Prawn Creole Casserole And Garlic Lemon Scallops ... 64
Tilapia Sandwiches With Tartar Sauce ... 64
Herb Lemon Mussels ... 65
Seafood Shrimp Omelet ... 65
Delicious Haddock ... 65
Lemony Prawns And Courgette ... 66
Tuna Patties ... 66

Snapper With Fruit	67
Italian Baked Cod	67
Breaded Scallops	67
Tender Juicy Honey Glazed Salmon	67
Fried Tilapia	68
Salmon Patties	68
Quick Easy Salmon	68
Fish Sandwich	69
Garlic Shrimp With Pasta Alfredo	69
Brown Sugar Garlic Salmon	70
Roasted Halibut Steaks With Parsley	70
Cajun Catfish Cakes With Cheese	70
Crispy Catfish	71
Salmon With Fennel Salad	71
Chicken Thighs With Brussels Sprouts	71
Sole And Cauliflower Fritters And Prawn Bake	72
Glazed Scallops	72
Honey Teriyaki Tilapia	72
"fried" Fish With Seasoned Potato Wedges	73
Coconut Cream Mackerel	73

Poultry Recipes 74

Asian Chicken Drumsticks	74
Ranch Turkey Tenders With Roasted Vegetable Salad	74
Thai Chicken With Cucumber And Chili Salad	75
Chicken And Potatoes	75
Nashville Hot Chicken	76
Crumbed Chicken Katsu	76
Almond Chicken	77
Cheddar-stuffed Chicken	77
Wild Rice And Kale Stuffed Chicken Thighs	77
Sweet-and-sour Chicken With Pineapple Cauliflower Rice	78
Wings With Corn On The Cob	78
Chicken Thighs In Waffles	79
Lemon-pepper Chicken Thighs With Buttery Roasted Radishes	79
Roasted Garlic Chicken Pizza With Cauliflower "wings"	80
Harissa-rubbed Chicken	80
Balsamic Duck Breast	81

Garlic Parmesan Drumsticks 81
Brazilian Chicken Drumsticks 81
Thai Curry Meatballs 82
Easy Chicken Thighs 82
Bacon Wrapped Stuffed Chicken 82
Crispy Dill Chicken Strips 83
Chicken Drumsticks 83
Chicken Leg Piece 83
Chicken & Veggies 84
Chicken Wings 84
Sweet And Spicy Carrots With Chicken Thighs 84
Easy Cajun Chicken Drumsticks 85
Italian Chicken & Potatoes 85
African Piri-piri Chicken Drumsticks 85
Bell Pepper Stuffed Chicken Roll-ups 86
Cajun Chicken With Vegetables 86
Marinated Chicken Legs 86
Air-fried Turkey Breast With Roasted Green Bean Casserole 87
Bruschetta Chicken 87
Barbecue Chicken Drumsticks With Crispy Kale Chips 88
Chicken Cordon Bleu 88
Air Fried Turkey Breast 89
Sesame Ginger Chicken 89

Desserts Recipes 89
Baked Brazilian Pineapple 89
Homemade Mint Pie And Strawberry Pecan Pie 90
Apple Wedges With Apricots And Coconut Mixed Berry Crisp 90
Bourbon Bread Pudding And Ricotta Lemon Poppy Seed Cake 91
Oreo Rolls 91
Strawberry Shortcake 92
Savory Almond Butter Cookie Balls 92
Cake In The Air Fryer 92
Pecan And Cherry Stuffed Apples 93
Cream Cheese Shortbread Cookies 93
Pumpkin-spice Bread Pudding 93
Crispy Pineapple Rings 94
Pumpkin Hand Pies Blueberry Hand Pies 94

Cinnamon-sugar "churros" With Caramel Sauce 95
Pineapple Wontons 95
Butter And Chocolate Chip Cookies 96
Lemon Raspberry Muffins 96
Sweet Potato Donut Holes 96
Banana Spring Rolls With Hot Fudge Dip 97
Fried Cheesecake Bites 97
Delicious Apple Fritters 98
Apple Crumble 98
Chocó Lava Cake 98
Biscuit Doughnuts 99
Chocolate Muffins 99
Soft Pecan Brownies 99
Lime Bars 100
Pecan Brownies And Cinnamon-sugar Almonds 100
Baked Apples 100
Churros 101
Gluten-free Spice Cookies 101
Healthy Semolina Pudding 101
Chocolate Mug Cakes 102

RECIPES INDEX **103**

MEASUREMENT CONVERSIONS

BASIC KITCHEN CONVERSIONS & EQUIVALENTS

DRY MEASUREMENTS CONVERSION CHART

3 TEASPOONS = 1 TABLESPOON = 1/16 CUP
6 TEASPOONS = 2 TABLESPOONS = 1/8 CUP
12 TEASPOONS = 4 TABLESPOONS = 1/4 CUP
24 TEASPOONS = 8 TABLESPOONS = 1/2 CUP
36 TEASPOONS = 12 TABLESPOONS = 3/4 CUP
48 TEASPOONS = 16 TABLESPOONS = 1 CUP

METRIC TO US COOKING CONVER-SIONS

OVEN TEMPERATURES

120 °C = 250 °F
160 °C = 320 °F
180 °C = 350 °F
205 °C = 400 °F
220 °C = 425 °F

LIQUID MEASUREMENTS CONVERSION CHART

8 FLUID OUNCES = 1 CUP = 1/2 PINT = 1/4 QUART
16 FLUID OUNCES = 2 CUPS = 1 PINT = 1/2 QUART
32 FLUID OUNCES = 4 CUPS = 2 PINTS = 1 QUART
1/4 GALLON
128 FLUID OUNCES = 16 CUPS = 8 PINTS = 4 QUARTS = 1 GALLON

BAKING IN GRAMS

1 CUP FLOUR = 140 GRAMS
1 CUP SUGAR = 150 GRAMS
1 CUP POWDERED SUGAR = 160 GRAMS
1 CUP HEAVY CREAM = 235 GRAMS

VOLUME

1 MILLILITER = 1/5 TEASPOON
5 ML = 1 TEASPOON
15 ML = 1 TABLESPOON
240 ML = 1 CUP OR 8 FLUID OUNCES
1 LITER = 34 FL. OUNCES

WEIGHT

1 GRAM = 035 OUNCES
100 GRAMS = 3.5 OUNCES
500 GRAMS = 1.1 POUNDS
1 KILOGRAM = 35 OUNCES

US TO METRIC COOKING CONVERSIONS

1/5 TSP = 1 ML
1 TSP=5 ML
1 TBSP = 15 ML
1 FL OUNCE = 30 ML
1 CUP=237 ML
1 PINT (2 CUPS) = 473 ML
1 QUART (4 CUPS)=.95 LITER
1GALLON (16 CUPS)=3.8LITERS
1 0Z=28 GRAMS
1 POUND = 454 GRAMS

BUTTER

1 CUP BUTTER=2 STICKS = 8 OUNCES = 230 GRAMS=8 TABLESPOONS

WHAT DOES 1 CUP EQUAL

1 CUP = 8 FLUID OUNCES
1 CUP = 16 TABLESPOONS
1 CUP = 48 TEASPOONS
1 CUP = 1/2 PINT
1 CUP = 1/4 QUART
1 CUP = 1/16 GALLON
1 CUP = 240 ML

BAKING PAN CONVERSIONS

1 CUP ALL-PURPOSE FLOUR=4.5 OZ
1 CUP ROLLED OATS = 3 OZ 1 LARGE EGG = 1.7 OZ
1 CUP BUTTER=8OZ 1 CUP MILK = 8 OZ
1 CUP HEAVY CREAM = 8.4 OZ
1 CUP GRANULATED SUGAR=7.1 OZ
1 CUP PACKED BROWN SUGAR = 7.75 OZ
1 CUP VEGETABLE OIL = 7.7 OZ
1 CUP UNSIFTED POWDERED SUGAR = 4.4 OZ

BAKING PAN CONVERSIONS

9-INCH ROUND CAKE PAN= 12 CUPS
10-INCH TUBE PAN =16 CUPS
11-INCH BUNDT PAN = 12 CUPS
9-INCH SPRINGFORM PAN = 10 CUPS
9 X 5 INCH LOAF PAN=8 CUPS
9-INCH SQUARE PAN=8 CUPS

Breakfast Recipes

French Toasts

Servings: 4
Cooking Time: 6 Minutes
Ingredients:
- 4 eggs
- 120g evaporated milk
- 6 tablespoons sugar
- 4 teaspoons olive oil
- ¼ teaspoon ground cinnamon
- ¼ teaspoon vanilla extract
- 8 bread slices

Directions:
1. Line each basket of "Zone 1" and "Zone 2" with a greased piece of foil.
2. Then Press your chosen zone - "Zone 1" or "Zone 2" and then rotate the knob to select "Air Fry".
3. Set the temperature to 200 degrees C and then set the time for 5 minutes to preheat.
4. In a large bowl, add all ingredients except for bread slices and beat until well combined.
5. Coat the bread slices with egg mixture evenly.
6. After preheating, arrange 4 bread slices into the basket of each zone.
7. Slide the basket into the Air Fryer and set the time for 6 minutes.
8. While cooking, flip the slices once halfway through.
9. After cooking time is completed, remove the French toasts from Air Fryer and serve warm.

Bacon, Cheese, And Avocado Melt & Cheesy Scrambled Eggs

Servings: 4
Cooking Time: 9 Minutes
Ingredients:
- Bacon, Cheese, and Avocado Melt:
- 1 avocado
- 4 slices cooked bacon, chopped
- 2 tablespoons salsa
- 1 tablespoon double cream
- 60 ml shredded Cheddar cheese
- Cheesy Scrambled Eggs:
- 1 teaspoon unsalted butter
- 2 large eggs
- 2 tablespoons milk
- 2 tablespoons shredded Cheddar cheese
- Salt and freshly ground black pepper, to taste

Directions:
1. Make the Bacon, Cheese, and Avocado Melt :
2. Preheat the zone 1 air fryer drawer to 204°C.
3. Slice the avocado in half lengthwise and remove the stone. To ensure the avocado halves do not roll in the drawer, slice a thin piece of skin off the base.
4. In a small bowl, combine the bacon, salsa, and cream. Divide the mixture between the avocado halves and top with the cheese.
5. Place the avocado halves in the zone 1 air fryer drawer and air fry for 3 to 5 minutes until the cheese has melted and begins to brown. Serve warm.
6. Make the Cheesy Scrambled Eggs :
7. Preheat the zone 2 air fryer drawer to 150°C. Place the butter in a baking pan and cook for 1 to 2 minutes, until melted.
8. In a small bowl, whisk together the eggs, milk, and cheese. Season with salt and black pepper. Transfer the mixture to the pan.
9. Cook for 3 minutes. Stir the eggs and push them toward the center of the pan.
10. Cook for another 2 minutes, then stir again. Cook for another 2 minutes, until the eggs are just cooked. Serve warm.

Easy Sausage Pizza

Servings: 4
Cooking Time: 6 Minutes
Ingredients:
- 2 tablespoons ketchup
- 1 pitta bread
- 80 ml sausage meat
- 230 g Mozzarella cheese
- 1 teaspoon garlic powder
- 1 tablespoon olive oil

Directions:
1. Preheat the air fryer to 170°C.
2. Spread the ketchup over the pitta bread.
3. Top with the sausage meat and cheese. Sprinkle with the garlic powder and olive oil.
4. Put the pizza in the zone 1 air fryer basket and bake for 6 minutes.
5. Serve warm.

Sausage And Egg Breakfast Burrito

Servings: 6
Cooking Time: 30 Minutes
Ingredients:
- 6 eggs
- Salt and pepper, to taste
- Cooking oil
- 120 ml chopped red pepper
- 120 ml chopped green pepper
- 230 g chicken sausage meat (removed from casings)
- 120 ml salsa
- 6 medium (8-inch) flour tortillas
- 120 ml shredded Cheddar cheese

Directions:
1. In a medium bowl, whisk the eggs. Add salt and pepper to taste.
2. Place a skillet on medium-high heat. Spray with cooking oil. Add the eggs. Scramble for 2 to 3 minutes, until the eggs are fluffy. Remove the eggs from the skillet and set aside.
3. If needed, spray the skillet with more oil. Add the chopped red and green bell peppers. Cook for 2 to 3 minutes, until the peppers are soft.
4. Add the sausage meat to the skillet. Break the sausage into smaller pieces using a spatula or spoon. Cook for 3 to 4 minutes, until the sausage is brown.
5. Add the salsa and scrambled eggs. Stir to combine. Remove the skillet from heat.
6. Spoon the mixture evenly onto the tortillas.
7. To form the burritos, fold the sides of each tortilla in toward the middle and then roll up from the bottom. You can secure each burrito with a toothpick. Or you can moisten the outside edge of the tortilla with a small amount of water. I prefer to use a cooking brush, but you can also dab with your fingers.
8. Spray the burritos with cooking oil and place them in the two air fryer drawers. Do not stack. Air fry at 204°C for 8 minutes.
9. Open the air fryer and flip the burritos. Cook for an additional 2 minutes or until crisp.
10. Sprinkle the Cheddar cheese over the burritos. Cool before serving.

Roasted Oranges

Servings: 4
Cooking Time: 6 Minutes
Ingredients:
- 2 oranges, halved
- 2 teaspoons honey
- 1 teaspoon cinnamon

Directions:
1. Place the oranges in each air fryer basket.
2. Drizzle honey and cinnamon over the orange halves.
3. Return the air fryer basket 1 to Zone 1, and basket 2 to Zone 2 of the Ninja Foodi 2-Basket Air Fryer.
4. Choose the "Air Fry" mode for Zone 1 at 395 degrees F temperature and 6 minutes of cooking time.
5. Select the "MATCH COOK" option to copy the settings for Zone 2.
6. Initiate cooking by pressing the START/PAUSE BUTTON.
7. Serve.

Nutrition:
- (Per serving) Calories 183 | Fat 15g |Sodium 402mg | Carbs 2.5g | Fiber 0.4g | Sugar 1.1g | Protein 10g

Savory Soufflé

Servings: 4
Cooking Time: 8 Minutes
Ingredients:
- 4 tablespoons light cream
- 4 eggs
- 2 tablespoons fresh parsley, chopped
- 2 fresh red chilies pepper, chopped
- Salt, as required

Directions:
1. In a bowl, add all the ingredients and beat until well combined.
2. Divide the mixture into 4 greased soufflé dishes.
3. Press either "Zone 1" and "Zone 2" of Ninja Foodi 2-Basket Air Fryer and then rotate the knob to select "Air Fry".
4. Set the temperature to 200 degrees C, and then set the time for 5 minutes to preheat.
5. After preheating, arrange soufflé dishes into the basket.
6. Slide basket into Air Fryer and set the time for 8 minutes.
7. After cooking time is completed, remove the soufflé dishes from Air Fryer and serve warm.

Glazed Apple Fritters Glazed Peach Fritters

Servings: 4
Cooking Time: 12 Minutes
Ingredients:
- FOR THE FRITTERS
- ¾ cup all-purpose flour
- 2 tablespoons granulated sugar
- 1 teaspoon baking powder
- ½ teaspoon kosher salt
- ½ teaspoon ground cinnamon
- ⅓ cup whole milk
- 2 tablespoons cold unsalted butter, grated
- 1 large egg
- 1 teaspoon fresh lemon juice
- 1 apple, peeled and diced
- 1 peach, peeled and diced
- FOR THE GLAZE
- ½ cup powdered sugar
- 1 tablespoon whole milk
- ½ teaspoon vanilla extract
- ½ teaspoon ground cinnamon
- Pinch salt

Directions:
1. To prep the fritters: In a large bowl, combine the flour, granulated sugar, baking powder, salt, and cinnamon. Stir in the milk, butter, egg, and lemon juice to form a thick batter.
2. Transfer half of the batter to a second bowl. Fold the apples into one bowl and the peaches into the other.
3. To prep the glaze: In a small bowl, whisk together the powdered sugar, milk, vanilla, cinnamon, and salt until smooth. Set aside.
4. To cook the fritters: Install a crisper plate in each of the two baskets. Drop two ¼-cup scoops of the apple fritter batter into the Zone 1 basket and insert the basket in the unit. Drop two ¼-cup scoops of the peach fritter batter into the Zone 2 basket and insert the basket in the unit.
5. Select Zone 1, select AIR FRY, set the temperature to 345°F, and set the time to 10 minutes.
6. Select Zone 2, select AIR FRY, set the temperature to 345°F, and set the time to 12 minutes. Select SMART FINISH.
7. Press START/PAUSE to begin cooking.
8. When cooking is complete, transfer the fritters to a wire rack and drizzle the glaze over them. Serve warm or at room temperature.

Nutrition:
- (Per serving) Calories: 298; Total fat: 8g; Saturated fat: 4.5g; Carbohydrates: 53g; Fiber: 3g; Protein: 5g; Sodium: 170mg

Mushroom-and-tomato Stuffed Hash Browns

Servings: 4
Cooking Time: 20 Minutes
Ingredients:
- Olive oil cooking spray
- 1 tablespoon plus 2 teaspoons olive oil, divided
- 110 g baby mushrooms, diced
- 1 spring onion, white parts and green parts, diced
- 1 garlic clove, minced
- 475 ml shredded potatoes
- ½ teaspoon salt
- ¼ teaspoon black pepper
- 1 plum tomato, diced
- 120 ml shredded mozzarella

Directions:
1. Lightly coat the inside of a 6-inch cake pan with olive oil cooking spray. In a small skillet, heat 2 teaspoons olive oil over medium heat. Add the mushrooms, spring onion, and garlic, and cook for 4 to 5 minutes, or until they have softened and are beginning to show some color.
2. Remove from heat. Meanwhile, in a large bowl, combine the potatoes, salt, pepper, and the remaining tablespoon olive oil. Toss until all potatoes are well coated. Pour half of the potatoes into the bottom of the cake pan.
3. Top with the mushroom mixture, tomato, and mozzarella. Spread the remaining potatoes over the top. Place the cake pan into the zone 1 drawer.
4. Select Bake button and adjust temperature to 190ºC, set time to 12 to 15 minutes and press Start. Until the top is golden brown, remove from the air fryer and allow to cool for 5 minutes before slicing and serving.

Cinnamon Toast

Servings: 6
Cooking Time: 5 Minutes
Ingredients:
- 12 slices bread
- 115g butter, at room temperature
- 100g white sugar
- 1½ teaspoons ground cinnamon
- 1½ teaspoons pure vanilla extract
- 1 pinch of salt

Directions:
1. Softened butter is mashed with a fork or the back of a spoon, and then sugar, cinnamon, vanilla, and salt are added.
2. Stir everything together thoroughly.
3. Spread one-sixth of the mixture onto each slice of bread, covering the entire surface.
4. Press your chosen zone - "Zone 1" or "Zone 2" and then rotate the knob to select "Air Fryer".
5. Set the temperature to 200 degrees C, and then set the time for 3 minutes to preheat.
6. After preheating, arrange bread into the basket of each zone.
7. Slide the basket into the Air Fryer and set the time for 5 minutes.
8. After cooking time is completed, remove both baskets from Air Fryer.
9. Cut bread slices diagonally and serve.

Potatoes Lyonnaise

Servings: 4
Cooking Time: 31 Minutes
Ingredients:
- 1 sweet/mild onion, sliced
- 1 teaspoon butter, melted
- 1 teaspoon brown sugar
- 2 large white potatoes (about 450 g in total), sliced ½-inch thick
- 1 tablespoon vegetable oil
- Salt and freshly ground black pepper, to taste

Directions:
1. Preheat the air fryer to 188°C.
2. Toss the sliced onions, melted butter and brown sugar together in the zone 1 air fryer drawer. Air fry for 8 minutes, shaking the drawer occasionally to help the onions cook evenly.
3. While the onions are cooking, bring a saucepan of salted water to a boil on the stovetop. Par-cook the potatoes in boiling water for 3 minutes. Drain the potatoes and pat them dry with a clean kitchen towel.
4. Add the potatoes to the onions in the zone 1 air fryer drawer and drizzle with vegetable oil. Toss to coat the potatoes with the oil and season with salt and freshly ground black pepper.
5. Increase the air fryer temperature to 204°C and air fry for 20 minutes, tossing the vegetables a few times during the cooking time to help the potatoes brown evenly.
6. Season with salt and freshly ground black pepper and serve warm.

Breakfast Casserole

Servings: 4
Cooking Time: 10
Ingredients:
- 1 pound of beef sausage, grounded
- 1/4 cup diced white onion
- 1 diced green bell pepper
- 8 whole eggs, beaten
- ½ cup Colby jack cheese, shredded
- ¼ teaspoon of garlic salt
- Oil spray, for greasing

Directions:
1. Take a bowl and add ground sausage to it.
2. Add in the diced onions, bell peppers, eggs and whisk it well.
3. Then season it with garlic salt.
4. Spray both the baskets of the air fryer with oil spray.
5. Divide this mixture among the baskets; remember to remove the crisper plates.
6. Top the mixture with cheese.
7. Now, turn ON the Ninja Foodie 2-Basket Air Fryer zone 1 and select AIR FRY mode and set the time to 10 minutes at 390 degrees F.
8. Select the MATCH button for zone 2 baskets, and hit start.
9. Once the cooking cycle completes, take out, and serve.
10. Serve and enjoy.

Nutrition:
- (Per serving) Calories 699| Fat 59.1g | Sodium 1217 mg | Carbs 6.8g | Fiber 0.6g| Sugar 2.5g | Protein 33.1 g

Bagels

Servings: 8
Cooking Time: 15 Minutes
Ingredients:
- 2 cups self-rising flour
- 2 cups non-fat plain Greek yogurt
- 2 beaten eggs for egg wash (optional)
- ½ cup sesame seeds (optional)

Directions:
1. In a medium mixing bowl, combine the self-rising flour and Greek yogurt using a wooden spoon.
2. Knead the dough for about 5 minutes on a lightly floured board.
3. Divide the dough into four equal pieces and roll each into a thin rope, securing the ends to form a bagel shape.
4. Install a crisper plate in both drawers. Place 4 bagels in a single layer in each drawer. Insert the drawers into the unit.
5. Select zone 1, select AIR FRY, set temperature to 360 degrees F/ 180 degrees C, and set time to 15 minutes. Select MATCH to match zone 2 settings to zone 1. Select START/STOP to begin.
6. Once the timer has finished, remove the bagels from the units.
7. Serve and enjoy!

Nutrition:
- (Per serving) Calories 202 | Fat 4.5g | Sodium 55mg | Carbs 31.3g | Fiber 2.7g | Sugar 4.7g | Protein 8.7g

Sausage With Eggs

Servings: 2
Cooking Time: 13
Ingredients:
- 4 sausage links, raw and uncooked
- 4 eggs, uncooked
- 1 tablespoon of green onion
- 2 tablespoons of chopped tomatoes
- Salt and black pepper, to taste
- 2 tablespoons of milk, dairy
- Oil spray, for greasing

Directions:
1. Take a bowl and whisk eggs in it.
2. Then pour milk, and add onions and tomatoes.
3. Whisk it all well.
4. Now season it with salt and black pepper.
5. Take one cake pan, that fit inside the air fryer and grease it with oil spray.
6. Pour the omelet in the greased cake pans.
7. Put the cake pan inside zone 1 air fryer basket of Ninja Foodie 2-Basket Air Fryer.
8. Now place the sausage link into the zone 2 basket.
9. Select bake for zone 1 basket and set the timer to 8-10 minutes at 300 degrees F.
10. For the zone 2 basket, select the AIR FRY button and set the timer to 12 minutes at 390 degrees.
11. Once the cooking cycle completes, serve by transferring it to plates.
12. Chop the sausage or cut it in round and then mix it with omelet.
13. Enjoy hot as a delicious breakfast.

Nutrition:
- (Per serving) Calories 240 | Fat 18.4g| Sodium 396mg | Carbs 2.8g | Fiber0.2g | Sugar 2g | Protein 15.6g

Sweet Potatoes Hash

Servings: 2
Cooking Time: 25
Ingredients:
- 450 grams sweet potatoes
- 1/2 white onion, diced
- 3 tablespoons of olive oil
- 1 teaspoon smoked paprika
- 1/4 teaspoon cumin
- 1/3 teaspoon of ground turmeric
- 1/4 teaspoon of garlic salt
- 1 cup guacamole

Directions:
1. Peel and cut the potatoes into cubes.
2. Now, transfer the potatoes to a bowl and add oil, white onions, cumin, paprika, turmeric, and garlic salt.
3. Put this mixture between both the baskets of the Ninja Foodie 2-Basket Air Fryer.
4. Set it to AIR FRY mode for 10 minutes at 390 degrees F.
5. Then take out the baskets and shake them well.
6. Then again set time to 15 minutes at 390 degrees F.
7. Once done, serve it with guacamole.

Nutrition:
- (Per serving) Calories691 | Fat 49.7g| Sodium 596mg | Carbs 64g | Fiber15g | Sugar 19g | Protein 8.1g

Banana And Raisins Muffins

Servings: 2
Cooking Time: 16
Ingredients:
- Salt, pinch
- 2 eggs, whisked
- 1/3 cup butter, melted
- 4 tablespoons of almond milk
- ¼ teaspoon of vanilla extract
- ½ teaspoon of baking powder
- 1-1/2 cup all-purpose flour
- 1 cup mashed bananas
- 2 tablespoons of raisins

Directions:
1. Take about 4 large (one-cup sized) ramekins and layer them with muffin papers.
2. Crack eggs in a large bowl, and whisk it all well and start adding vanilla extract, almond milk, baking powder, and melted butter.
3. Whisk the ingredients very well.
4. Take a separate bowl and add the all-purpose flour, and salt.
5. Now, combine the add dry ingredients with the wet ingredients.
6. Now, pour mashed bananas and raisins into this batter
7. Mix it well to make a batter for the muffins.
8. Now pour the batter into four ramekins and divided the ramekins in the air fryer zones.
9. Set the timer for zone 1 to 16 minutes at 350 degrees F.
10. Select the MATCH button for the zone 2 basket.
11. Check if not done, and let it AIR FRY for one more minute.
12. Once it is done, serve.

Nutrition:
- (Per serving) Calories 727| Fat 43.1g| Sodium 366 mg | Carbs 74.4g | Fiber 4.7g | Sugar 16.1g | Protein 14.1g

Puff Pastry

Servings: 6
Cooking Time: 10 Minutes
Ingredients:
- 1 package (200g) cream cheese, softened
- 50g sugar
- 2 tablespoons plain flour
- ½ teaspoon vanilla extract
- 2 large egg yolks
- 1 tablespoon water
- 1 package frozen puff pastry, thawed
- 210g seedless raspberry jam

Directions:
1. Mix the cream cheese, sugar, flour, and vanilla extract until smooth, then add 1 egg yolk.
2. Combine the remaining egg yolk with the water. Unfold each sheet of puff pastry on a lightly floured board and roll into a 30 cm square. Cut into nine 10 cm squares.
3. Put 1 tablespoon cream cheese mixture and 1 rounded teaspoon jam on each. Bring 2 opposite corners of pastry over filling, sealing with yolk mixture.
4. Brush the remaining yolk mixture over the tops.
5. Press your chosen zone - "Zone 1" or "Zone 2" and then rotate the knob to select "Air Fry".
6. Set the temperature to 160 degrees C, and then set the time for 5 minutes to preheat.
7. After preheating, spray the Air-Fryer basket of each zone with cooking spray, line them with parchment paper, and place the pastry on them.
8. Slide the basket into the Air Fryer and set the time for 10 minutes.
9. After cooking time is completed, transfer them onto serving plates and serve.

Sausage And Cheese Balls

Servings: 16 Balls
Cooking Time: 12 Minutes
Ingredients:
- 450 g pork sausage meat, removed from casings
- 120 ml shredded Cheddar cheese
- 30 g full-fat cream cheese, softened
- 1 large egg

Directions:
1. Mix all ingredients in a large bowl. Form into sixteen balls. Place the balls into the two air fryer drawers.
2. Adjust the temperature to 204°C and air fry for 12 minutes.
3. Shake the drawers two or three times during cooking. Sausage balls will be browned on the outside and have an internal temperature of at least 64°C when completely cooked.
4. Serve warm.

Banana Bread

Servings: 8
Cooking Time: 35 Minutes
Ingredients:
- 95g flour
- 1 teaspoon ground cinnamon
- ¼ teaspoon ground nutmeg
- ½ teaspoon salt
- ¼ teaspoon baking soda
- 2 medium-sized ripe bananas mashed
- 2 large eggs lightly beaten
- 100g granulated sugar
- 2 tablespoons whole milk
- 1 tablespoon plain nonfat yoghurt
- 2 tablespoons vegetable oil
- 1 teaspoon vanilla
- 2 tablespoons walnuts roughly chopped

Directions:
1. Combine flour, cinnamon, nutmeg, baking soda, and salt in a large mixing basin.
2. Mash the banana in a separate dish before adding the eggs, sugar, milk, yoghurt, oil, and vanilla extract.
3. Combine the wet and dry ingredients in a mixing bowl and stir until just incorporated.
4. Pour the batter into the loaf pan and top with chopped walnuts.
5. Press either "Zone 1" and "Zone 2" and then rotate the knob select "Air Fryer".
6. Set the temperature to 155 degrees C, and then set the time for 3 minutes to preheat.
7. After preheating, arrange 1 loaf pan into the basket.
8. Slide basket into Air Fryer and set the time for 35 minutes.
9. After cooking time is completed, remove pan from Air Fryer.
10. Place the loaf pan onto a wire rack to cool for about 10 minutes.
11. Carefully invert the bread onto a wire rack to cool completely before slicing
12. Cut the bread into desired-sized slices and serve.

Cinnamon-raisin Bagels Everything Bagels

Servings: 4
Cooking Time: 14 Minutes
Ingredients:
- FOR THE BAGEL DOUGH
- 1 cup all-purpose flour, plus more for dusting
- 2 teaspoons baking powder
- 1 teaspoon kosher salt
- 1 cup reduced-fat plain Greek yogurt
- FOR THE CINNAMON-RAISIN BAGELS
- ¼ cup raisins
- ½ teaspoon ground cinnamon
- FOR THE EVERYTHING BAGELS
- ¼ teaspoon poppy seeds
- ¼ teaspoon sesame seeds
- ¼ teaspoon dried minced garlic
- ¼ teaspoon dried minced onion
- FOR THE EGG WASH
- 1 large egg
- 1 tablespoon water

Directions:
1. To prep the bagels: In a large bowl, combine the flour, baking powder, and salt. Stir in the yogurt to form a soft dough. Turn the dough out onto a lightly floured surface and knead five to six times, until it is smooth and elastic. Divide the dough in half.
2. Knead the raisins and cinnamon into one dough half. Leave the other dough half plain.
3. Divide both portions of dough in half to form a total of 4 balls of dough (2 cinnamon-raisin and 2 plain). Roll each ball of dough into a rope about 8 inches long. Shape each rope into a ring and pinch the ends to seal.
4. To prep the everything bagels: In a small bowl, mix together the poppy seeds, sesame seeds, garlic, and onion.
5. To prep the egg wash: In a second small bowl, beat together the egg and water. Brush the egg wash on top of each bagel.
6. Generously sprinkle the everything seasoning over the top of the 2 plain bagels.
7. To cook the bagels: Install a crisper plate in each of the two baskets. Place the cinnamon-raisin bagels in the Zone 1 basket and insert the basket in the unit. For best results, the bagels should not overlap in the basket. Place the everything bagels in the Zone 2 basket and insert the basket in the unit.
8. Select Zone 1, select AIR FRY, set the temperature to 325°F, and set the time to 14 minutes. Select MATCH COOK to match Zone 2 settings to Zone 1.
9. Press START/PAUSE to begin cooking.
10. When cooking is complete, use silicone-tipped tongs to transfer the bagels to a cutting board. Let cool for 2 to 3 minutes before cutting and serving.

Nutrition:
- (Per serving) Calories: 238; Total fat: 3g; Saturated fat: 1g; Carbohydrates: 43g; Fiber: 1.5g; Protein: 11g; Sodium: 321mg

Sausage Hash And Baked Eggs

Servings: 4
Cooking Time: 30 Minutes
Ingredients:
- FOR THE HASH
- 2 yellow potatoes (about 1 pound), cut into ½-inch pieces
- 4 garlic cloves, minced
- 1 teaspoon kosher salt
- ¼ teaspoon freshly ground black pepper
- 2 tablespoons olive oil
- ½ pound pork breakfast sausage meat
- 1 small yellow onion, diced
- 1 red bell pepper, diced
- 1 teaspoon Italian seasoning
- FOR THE EGGS
- Nonstick cooking spray
- 4 large eggs
- 4 tablespoons water

Directions:
1. To prep the hash: In a large bowl, combine the potatoes, garlic, salt, black pepper, and olive oil and toss to coat. Crumble in the sausage and mix until combined.
2. To prep the eggs: Mist 4 silicone muffin cups with cooking spray. Crack 1 egg into each muffin cup. Top each egg with 1 tablespoon of water.
3. To cook the hash and eggs: Install a crisper plate in the Zone 1 basket. Place the sausage and potato mixture in the Zone 1 basket and insert the basket in the unit. Place the egg cups in the Zone 2 basket and insert the basket in the unit.
4. Select Zone 1, select AIR FRY, set the temperature to 400°F, and set the time to 30 minutes.
5. Select Zone 2, select BAKE, set the temperature to 325°F, and set the time to 12 minutes. Select SMART FINISH.
6. Press START/PAUSE to begin cooking.
7. When the Zone 1 timer reads 20 minutes, press START/PAUSE. Remove the basket and add the onion, bell pepper, and Italian seasoning to the hash. Mix until combined, breaking up any large pieces of sausage. Reinsert the basket and press START/PAUSE to resume cooking.
8. When cooking is complete, serve the hash topped with an egg.

Nutrition:
- (Per serving) Calories: 400; Total fat: 23g; Saturated fat: 5.5g; Carbohydrates: 31g; Fiber: 2g; Protein: 19g; Sodium: 750mg

Egg With Baby Spinach

Servings: 4
Cooking Time: 12
Ingredients:
- Nonstick spray, for greasing ramekins
- 2 tablespoons olive oil
- 6 ounces baby spinach
- 2 garlic cloves, minced
- 1/3 teaspoon kosher salt
- 6-8 large eggs
- ½ cup half and half
- Salt and black pepper, to taste
- 8 Sourdough bread slices, toasted

Directions:
1. Grease 4 ramekins with oil spray and set aside for further use.
2. Take a skillet and heat oil in it.
3. Then cook spinach for 2 minutes and add garlic and salt black pepper.
4. Let it simmer for 2 more minutes.
5. Once the spinach is wilted, transfer it to a plate.
6. Whisk an egg into a small bowl.
7. Add in the spinach.
8. Whisk it well and then pour half and half.
9. Divide this mixture between 4 ramekins and remember not to overfill it to the top, leave a little space on top.
10. Put the ramekins in zone 1 and zone 2 baskets of the Ninja Foodie 2-Basket Air Fryer.
11. Press start and set zone 1 to AIR fry it at 350 degrees F for 8-12 minutes.
12. Press the MATCH button for zone 2.
13. Once it's cooked and eggs are done, serve with sourdough bread slices.

Nutrition:
- (Per serving) Calories 404| Fat 19.6g| Sodium 761mg | Carbs 40.1g | Fiber 2.5g| Sugar 2.5g | Protein 19.2g

Egg In Bread Hole

Servings: 1
Cooking Time: 8 Minutes
Ingredients:
- 1 tablespoon butter, softened
- 2 eggs
- 2 slices of bread
- Salt and black pepper, to taste

Directions:
1. Line either basket of "Zone 1" and "Zone 2" with a greased piece of foil.
2. Press your chosen zone - "Zone 1" or "Zone 2" and then rotate the knob to select "Air Fryer".
3. Set the temperature to 160 degrees C, and then set the time for 3 minutes to preheat.
4. After preheating, place the butter on both sides of the bread. Cut a hole in the centre of the bread and crack the egg.
5. Slide the basket into the Air Fryer and set the time for 6 minutes.
6. After cooking time is completed, transfer the bread to a serving plate and serve.

Blueberry Coffee Cake And Maple Sausage Patties

Servings: 6
Cooking Time: 25 Minutes
Ingredients:
- FOR THE COFFEE CAKE
- 6 tablespoons unsalted butter, at room temperature, divided
- ⅓ cup granulated sugar
- 1 large egg
- 1 teaspoon vanilla extract
- ¼ cup whole milk
- 1½ cups all-purpose flour, divided
- 1 teaspoon baking powder
- ¼ teaspoon salt
- 1 cup blueberries
- ¼ cup packed light brown sugar
- ½ teaspoon ground cinnamon
- FOR THE SAUSAGE PATTIES
- ½ pound ground pork
- 2 tablespoons maple syrup
- ½ teaspoon dried sage
- ½ teaspoon dried thyme
- 1½ teaspoons kosher salt
- ½ teaspoon crushed fennel seeds
- ½ teaspoon red pepper flakes (optional)
- ¼ teaspoon freshly ground black pepper

Directions:
1. To prep the coffee cake: In a large bowl, cream together 4 tablespoons of butter with the granulated sugar. Beat in the egg, vanilla, and milk.
2. Stir in 1 cup of flour, along with the baking soda and salt, to form a thick batter. Fold in the blueberries.
3. In a second bowl, mix the remaining 2 tablespoons of butter, remaining ½ cup of flour, the brown sugar, and cinnamon to form a dry crumbly mixture.
4. To prep the sausage patties: In a large bowl, mix the pork, maple syrup, sage, thyme, salt, fennel seeds, red pepper flakes (if using), and black pepper until just combined.
5. Divide the mixture into 6 equal patties about ½ inch thick.
6. To cook the coffee cake and sausage patties: Spread the cake batter into the Zone 1 basket, top with the crumble mixture, and insert the basket in the unit. Install a crisper plate in the Zone 2 basket, add the sausage patties in a single layer, and insert the basket in the unit.
7. Select Zone 1, select BAKE, set the temperature to 350°F, and set the time to 25 minutes.
8. Select Zone 2, select AIR FRY, set the temperature to 375°F, and set the time to 12 minutes. Select SMART FINISH.
9. Press START/PAUSE to begin cooking.
10. When the Zone 2 timer reads 6 minutes, press START/PAUSE. Remove the basket and use silicone-tipped tongs to flip the sausage patties. Reinsert the basket and press START/PAUSE to resume cooking.
11. When cooking is complete, let the coffee cake cool for at least 5 minutes, then cut into 6 slices. Serve warm or at room temperature with the sausage patties.

Nutrition:
- (Per serving) Calories: 395; Total fat: 15g; Saturated fat: 8g; Carbohydrates: 53g; Fiber: 1.5g; Protein: 14g; Sodium: 187mg

Buttermilk Biscuits With Roasted Stone Fruit Compote

Servings: 4
Cooking Time: 20 Minutes
Ingredients:
- FOR THE BISCUITS
- 1⅓ cups all-purpose flour
- 2 teaspoons sugar
- 2 teaspoons baking powder
- ½ teaspoon baking soda
- ½ teaspoon kosher salt
- 4 tablespoons (½ stick) very cold unsalted butter
- ½ cup plus 1 tablespoon low-fat buttermilk
- FOR THE FRUIT COMPOTE
- 2 peaches, peeled and diced
- 2 plums, peeled and diced
- ¼ cup water
- 2 teaspoons honey
- ⅛ teaspoon ground ginger (optional)

Directions:
1. To prep the biscuits: In a small bowl, combine the flour, sugar, baking powder, baking soda, and salt. Using the large holes on a box grater, grate in the butter. Stir in the buttermilk to form a thick dough.
2. Place the dough on a lightly floured surface and gently pat it into a ½-inch-thick disc. Fold the dough in half, then rotate the whole thing 90 degrees, pat into a ½-inch thick disc and fold again. Repeat until you have folded the dough four times.
3. Pat the dough out a final time into a ½-inch-thick disc and use a 3-inch biscuit cutter to cut 4 biscuits from the dough (discard the scraps).
4. To prep the fruit compote: In a large bowl, stir together the peaches, plums, water, honey, and ginger (if using).
5. To cook the biscuits and compote: Install a crisper plate in the Zone 1 basket, place the biscuits in the basket, and insert the basket in the unit. Place the fruit in the Zone 2 basket and insert the basket in the unit.
6. Select Zone 1, select AIR FRY, set the temperature to 400°F, and set the time to 10 minutes.
7. Select Zone 2, select ROAST, set the temperature to 350°F, and set the time to 20 minutes. Select SMART FINISH.
8. Press START/PAUSE to begin cooking.
9. When the Zone 2 timer reads 10 minutes, press START/PAUSE. Remove the basket and stir the compote. Reinsert the basket and press START/PAUSE to resume cooking.
10. When cooking is complete, the biscuits will be golden brown and crisp on top and the fruit will be soft. Transfer the biscuits to a plate to cool. Lightly mash the fruit to form a thick, jammy sauce.
11. Split the biscuits in half horizontally and serve topped with fruit compote.

Nutrition:
- (Per serving) Calories: 332; Total fat: 12g; Saturated fat: 7.5g; Carbohydrates: 50g; Fiber: 2.5g; Protein: 6g; Sodium: 350mg

Simple Bagels

Servings: 4
Cooking Time: 12 Minutes
Ingredients:
- 125g plain flour
- 2 teaspoons baking powder
- Salt, as required
- 240g plain Greek yogurt
- 1 egg, beaten
- 1 tablespoon water
- 1 tablespoon sesame seeds
- 1 teaspoon coarse salt

Directions:
1. In a large bowl, mix together the flour, baking powder and salt.
2. Add the yogurt and mix until a dough ball forms.
3. Place the dough onto a lightly floured surface and then cut into 4 equal-sized balls.
4. Roll each ball into a 17 – 19 cm rope and then join ends to shape a bagel.
5. Grease basket of Ninja Foodi 2-Basket Air Fryer.
6. Press your chosen zone - "Zone 1" or "Zone 2" and then rotate the knob to select "Air Fry".
7. Set the temperature to 165 degrees C and then set the time for 5 minutes to preheat.
8. Meanwhile, in a small bowl, add egg and water and mix well.
9. Brush the bagels with egg mixture evenly.
10. Sprinkle the top of each bagel with sesame seeds and salt, pressing lightly.
11. After preheating, arrange 2 bagels into the basket of each zone.
12. Slide the basket into the Air Fryer and set the time for 12 minutes.
13. After cooking time is completed, remove the bagels from Air Fryer and serve warm.

Breakfast Bacon

Servings: 4
Cooking Time: 14 Minutes.
Ingredients:
- ½ lb. bacon slices

Directions:
1. Spread half of the bacon slices in each of the crisper plate evenly in a single layer.
2. Return the crisper plate to the Ninja Foodi Dual Zone Air Fryer.
3. Choose the Air Fry mode for Zone 1 and set the temperature to 390 degrees F and the time to 14 minutes.
4. Select the "MATCH" button to copy the settings for Zone 2.
5. Initiate cooking by pressing the START/STOP button.
6. Flip the crispy bacon once cooked halfway through, then resume cooking.
7. Serve.

Nutrition:
- (Per serving) Calories 273 | Fat 22g |Sodium 517mg | Carbs 3.3g | Fiber 0.2g | Sugar 1.4g | Protein 16.1g

Cauliflower Avocado Toast And All-in-one Toast

Servings: 3
Cooking Time: 10 Minutes
Ingredients:
- Cauliflower Avocado Toast:
- 1 (40 g) steamer bag cauliflower
- 1 large egg
- 120 ml shredded Mozzarella cheese
- 1 ripe medium avocado
- ½ teaspoon garlic powder
- ¼ teaspoon ground black pepper
- All-in-One Toast:
- 1 strip bacon, diced
- 1 slice 1-inch thick bread
- 1 egg
- Salt and freshly ground black pepper, to taste
- 60 ml grated Monterey Jack or Chedday cheese

Directions:
1. Make the Cauliflower Avocado Toast :
2. Cook cauliflower according to package instructions. Remove from bag and place into cheesecloth or clean towel to remove excess moisture.
3. Place cauliflower into a large bowl and mix in egg and Mozzarella. Cut a piece of parchment to fit your air fryer drawer. Separate the cauliflower mixture into two, and place it on the parchment in two mounds. Press out the cauliflower mounds into a ¼-inch-thick rectangle. Place the parchment into the zone 1 air fryer drawer.
4. Adjust the temperature to 204°C and set the timer for 8 minutes.
5. Flip the cauliflower halfway through the cooking time.
6. When the timer beeps, remove the parchment and allow the cauliflower to cool 5 minutes.
7. Cut open the avocado and remove the pit. Scoop out the inside, place it in a medium bowl, and mash it with garlic powder and pepper. Spread onto the cauliflower. Serve immediately.
8. Make the All-in-One Toast :
9. Preheat the zone 2 air fryer drawer to 204°C.
10. Air fry the bacon for 3 minutes, shaking the zone 2 drawer once or twice while it cooks. Remove the bacon to a paper towel lined plate and set aside.
11. Use a sharp paring knife to score a large circle in the middle of the slice of bread, cutting halfway through, but not all the way through to the cutting board. Press down on the circle in the center of the bread slice to create an indentation.
12. Transfer the slice of bread, hole side up, to the air fryer drawer. Crack the egg into the center of the bread, and season with salt and pepper.
13. Adjust the air fryer temperature to 192°C and air fry for 5 minutes. Sprinkle the grated cheese around the edges of the bread, leaving the center of the yolk uncovered, and top with the cooked bacon. Press the cheese and bacon into the bread lightly to help anchor it to the bread and prevent it from blowing around in the air fryer.
14. Air fry for one or two more minutes, just to melt the cheese and finish cooking the egg. Serve immediately.

Parmesan Sausage Egg Muffins

Servings: 4
Cooking Time: 20 Minutes
Ingredients:
- 170 g Italian-seasoned sausage, sliced
- 6 eggs
- 30 ml double cream
- Salt and ground black pepper, to taste
- 85 g Parmesan cheese, grated

Directions:
1. Preheat the air fryer to 176°C. Grease a muffin pan.
2. Put the sliced sausage in the muffin pan.
3. Beat the eggs with the cream in a bowl and season with salt and pepper.
4. Pour half of the mixture over the sausages in the pan.
5. Sprinkle with cheese and the remaining egg mixture.
6. Bake in the preheated air fryer for 20 minutes or until set.
7. Serve immediately.

Cheesy Baked Eggs

Servings: 4
Cooking Time: 16 Minutes
Ingredients:
- 4 large eggs
- 57g smoked gouda, shredded
- Everything bagel seasoning, to taste
- Salt and pepper to taste

Directions:
1. Crack one egg in each ramekin.
2. Top the egg with bagel seasoning, black pepper, salt and gouda.
3. Place 2 ramekins in each air fryer basket.
4. Return the air fryer basket 1 to Zone 1, and basket 2 to Zone 2 of the Ninja Foodi 2-Basket Air Fryer.
5. Choose the "Air Fry" mode for Zone 1 and set the temperature to 400 degrees F and 16 minutes of cooking time.
6. Select the "MATCH COOK" option to copy the settings for Zone 2.
7. Initiate cooking by pressing the START/PAUSE BUTTON.
8. Serve warm.

Nutrition:
- (Per serving) Calories 190 | Fat 18g |Sodium 150mg | Carbs 0.6g | Fiber 0.4g | Sugar 0.4g | Protein 7.2g

Parmesan Ranch Risotto And Oat And Chia Porridge

Servings: 6
Cooking Time: 30 Minutes
Ingredients:
- Parmesan Ranch Risotto:
- 1 tablespoon olive oil
- 1 clove garlic, minced
- 1 tablespoon unsalted butter
- 1 onion, diced
- 180 ml Arborio rice
- 475 ml chicken stock, boiling
- 120 ml Parmesan cheese, grated
- Oat and Chia Porridge:
- 2 tablespoons peanut butter
- 4 tablespoons honey
- 1 tablespoon butter, melted
- 1 L milk
- 475 ml oats
- 235 ml chia seeds

Directions:
1. Make the Parmesan Ranch Risotto :
2. Preheat the air fryer to 200°C.
3. Grease a round baking tin with olive oil and stir in the garlic, butter, and onion.
4. Transfer the tin to the zone 1 air fryer basket and bake for 4 minutes. Add the rice and bake for 4 more minutes.
5. Turn the air fryer to 160°C and pour in the chicken stock. Cover and bake for 22 minutes.
6. Scatter with cheese and serve.
7. Make the Oat and Chia Porridge :
8. Preheat the air fryer to 200°C.
9. Put the peanut butter, honey, butter, and milk in a bowl and stir to mix. Add the oats and chia seeds and stir.
10. Transfer the mixture to a bowl and bake in the zone 2 air fryer basket for 5 minutes. Give another stir before serving.

Strawberry Baked Oats Chocolate Peanut Butter Baked Oats

Servings: 12
Cooking Time: 15 Minutes
Ingredients:
- FOR THE STRAWBERRY OATS
- 1 cup whole milk
- 1 cup heavy (whipping) cream
- ½ cup maple syrup
- 2 teaspoons vanilla extract
- 2 large eggs
- 2 cups old-fashioned oats
- 2 teaspoons baking powder
- ½ teaspoon ground cinnamon
- ¼ teaspoon kosher salt
- 1½ cups diced strawberries
- FOR THE CHOCOLATE PEANUT BUTTER OATS
- 2 very ripe bananas
- ½ cup maple syrup
- ¼ cup unsweetened cocoa powder
- 2 teaspoons vanilla extract
- 2 teaspoons baking powder
- 2 large eggs
- ½ teaspoon kosher salt
- 2 cups old-fashioned oats
- 2 tablespoons peanut butter

Directions:
1. To prep the strawberry oats: In a large bowl, combine the milk, cream, maple syrup, vanilla, and eggs. Stir in the oats, baking powder, cinnamon, and salt until fully combined. Fold in the strawberries.
2. To prep the chocolate peanut butter oats: In a large bowl, mash the banana with a fork. Stir in the maple syrup, cocoa powder, vanilla, baking powder, and salt until smooth. Beat in the eggs. Stir in the oats until everything is combined.
3. To bake the oats: Place the strawberry oatmeal in the Zone 1 basket and insert the basket in the unit. Place the chocolate peanut butter oatmeal in the Zone 2 basket. Add ½ teaspoon dollops of peanut butter on top and insert the basket in the unit.
4. Select Zone 1, select BAKE, set the temperature to 320°F, and set the time to 15 minutes. Select MATCH COOK to match Zone 2 settings to Zone 1.
5. Press START/PAUSE to begin cooking.
6. When cooking is complete, serve each oatmeal in a shallow bowl.

Nutrition:
- (Per serving) Calories: 367; Total fat: 19g; Saturated fat: 11g; Carbohydrates: 42g; Fiber: 3.5g; Protein: 8g; Sodium: 102mg

Breakfast Potatoes

Servings: 6
Cooking Time: 20 Minutes
Ingredients:
- 3 russet potatoes, cut into bite-sized pieces with skin on
- 1 teaspoon garlic powder
- 1 teaspoon onion powder
- 2 teaspoons fine ground sea salt
- 1 teaspoon black pepper
- 1 tablespoon olive oil
- ½ red pepper, diced

Directions:
1. The potatoes should be washed and scrubbed before being sliced into bite-sized pieces with the skin on.
2. Using paper towels, dry them and place them in a large mixing bowl.
3. Toss in the spices and drizzle with olive oil. Stir in the pepper until everything is completely combined.
4. Line a basket with parchment paper.
5. Press either "Zone 1" or "Zone 2" and then rotate the knob to select "Air Fryer".
6. Set the temperature to 195 degrees C, and then set the time for 3 minutes to preheat.
7. After preheating, spread the potatoes in a single layer on the sheet.
8. Slide basket into Air Fryer and set the time for 15 minutes.
9. After cooking time is completed, remove basket from Air Fryer.
10. Place them on serving plates and serve.

Easy Pancake Doughnuts

Servings: 8
Cooking Time: 9 Minutes
Ingredients:
- 2 eggs
- 50g sugar
- 125ml vegetable oil
- 240g pancake mix
- 1 ½ tbsp cinnamon

Directions:
1. In a bowl, mix pancake mix, eggs, cinnamon, sugar, and oil until well combined.
2. Pour the doughnut mixture into the silicone doughnut moulds.
3. Insert a crisper plate in Ninja Foodi air fryer baskets.
4. Place doughnut moulds in both baskets.
5. Select zone 1 then select "air fry" mode and set the temperature to 355 degrees F for 9 minutes. Press "match" to match zone 2 settings to zone 1. Press "start/stop" to begin.

Nutrition:
- (Per serving) Calories 163 | Fat 14.7g |Sodium 16mg | Carbs 7.4g | Fiber 0.7g | Sugar 6.4g | Protein 1.4g

Spinach Omelet And Bacon, Egg, And Cheese Roll Ups

Servings: 6
Cooking Time: 15 Minutes
Ingredients:
- Spinach Omelet:
- 4 large eggs
- 350 ml chopped fresh spinach leaves
- 2 tablespoons peeled and chopped brown onion
- 2 tablespoons salted butter, melted
- 120 ml shredded mild Cheddar cheese
- ¼ teaspoon salt
- Bacon, Egg, and Cheese Roll Ups:
- 2 tablespoons unsalted butter
- 60 ml chopped onion
- ½ medium green pepper, seeded and chopped
- 6 large eggs
- 12 slices bacon
- 235 ml shredded sharp Cheddar cheese
- 120 ml mild salsa, for dipping

Directions:
1. Make the Spinach Omelet :
2. In an ungreased round nonstick baking dish, whisk eggs. Stir in spinach, onion, butter, Cheddar, and salt.
3. Place dish into zone 1 air fryer basket. Adjust the temperature to 160°C and bake for 12 minutes. Omelet will be done when browned on the top and firm in the middle.
4. Slice in half and serve warm on two medium plates.
5. Make the Bacon, Egg, and Cheese Roll Ups :
6. In a medium skillet over medium heat, melt butter. Add onion and pepper to the skillet and sauté until fragrant and onions are translucent, about 3 minutes.
7. Whisk eggs in a small bowl and pour into skillet. Scramble eggs with onions and peppers until fluffy and fully cooked, about 5 minutes. Remove from heat and set aside.
8. On work surface, place three slices of bacon side by side, overlapping about ¼ inch. Place 60 ml scrambled eggs in a heap on the side closest to you and sprinkle 60 ml cheese on top of the eggs.
9. Tightly roll the bacon around the eggs and secure the seam with a toothpick if necessary. Place each roll into the zone 2 air fryer basket.
10. Adjust the temperature to 175°C and air fry for 15 minutes. Rotate the rolls halfway through the cooking time.
11. Bacon will be brown and crispy when completely cooked. Serve immediately with salsa for dipping.

Breakfast Pitta

Servings: 2
Cooking Time: 6 Minutes
Ingredients:
- 1 wholemeal pitta
- 2 teaspoons olive oil
- ½ shallot, diced
- ¼ teaspoon garlic, minced
- 1 large egg
- ¼ teaspoon dried oregano
- ¼ teaspoon dried thyme
- ⅛ teaspoon salt
- 2 tablespoons shredded Parmesan cheese

Directions:
1. Brush the top of the pitta with olive oil, then spread the diced shallot and minced garlic over the pitta. Crack the egg into a small bowl or ramekin, and season it with oregano, thyme, and salt.
2. Place the pitta into the zone 1 drawer, and gently pour the egg onto the top of the pitta. Sprinkle with cheese over the top.
3. Select Bake button and adjust temperature to 190°C, set time to 6 minutes and press Start. After the end, allow to cool for 5 minutes before cutting into pieces for serving.

French Toast Sticks

Servings: 5
Cooking Time: 12 Minutes
Ingredients:
- 10 teaspoons sugar, divided
- 3¼ teaspoons cinnamon, divided
- 3 slices toast
- 1 egg
- 1 egg yolks
- 80ml milk
- 1 teaspoon sugar
- 1 teaspoon brown sugar
- 1 teaspoon vanilla
- ¼ teaspoon cinnamon

Directions:
1. Line either basket "Zone 1" and "Zone 2" with a greased piece of foil.
2. Press your chosen zone - "Zone 1" and "Zone 2" and then rotate the knob to select "Air Fryer".
3. Set the temperature to 175 degrees C, and then set the time for 3 minutes to preheat.
4. Three teaspoons of sugar and 3 teaspoons of cinnamon are whisked together in a shallow bowl. Set aside.
5. Cut each slice of bread in thirds.
6. Combine the eggs, egg yolks, milk, brown sugar, remaining sugar, vanilla, and remaining cinnamon in a shallow pan.
7. Blend everything until it's smooth.
8. Allow the bread to soak in the egg mixture for a few seconds. Flip over and dip the other side.
9. Coat both sides of the bread in the cinnamon-sugar mixture. Place in the basket.
10. Slide the basket into the Air Fryer and set the time for 8 minutes.
11. After cooking time is completed, transfer the bread to a serving plate and serve.

Canadian Bacon Muffin Sandwiches And All-in-one Toast

Servings: 5
Cooking Time: 10 Minutes
Ingredients:
- Canadian Bacon Muffin Sandwiches:
- 4 English muffins, split
- 8 slices back bacon
- 4 slices cheese
- Cooking spray
- All-in-One Toast:
- 1 strip bacon, diced
- 1 slice 1-inch thick bread
- 1 egg
- Salt and freshly ground black pepper, to taste
- 60 ml grated Monterey Jack or Chedday cheese

Directions:
1. Make the Canadian Bacon Muffin Sandwiches :
2. 1. Preheat the air fryer to 190°C. Make the sandwiches: Top each of 4 muffin halves with 2 slices of bacon, 1 slice of cheese, and finish with the remaining muffin half. 3. Put the sandwiches in the zone 1 air fryer basket and spritz the tops with cooking spray. 4. Bake for 4 minutes. Flip the sandwiches and bake for another 4 minutes. 5. Divide the sandwiches among four plates and serve warm.
3. Make the All-in-One Toast :
4. Preheat the air fryer to 205°C.
5. Air fry the bacon in zone 2 basket for 3 minutes, shaking the basket once or twice while it cooks. Remove the bacon to a paper towel lined plate and set aside.
6. Use a sharp paring knife to score a large circle in the middle of the slice of bread, cutting halfway through, but not all the way through to the cutting board. Press down on the circle in the center of the bread slice to create an indentation.
7. Transfer the slice of bread, hole side up, to the zone 2 air fryer basket. Crack the egg into the center of the bread, and season with salt and pepper.
8. Adjust the air fryer temperature to 190°C and air fry for 5 minutes. Sprinkle the grated cheese around the edges of the bread, leaving the center of the yolk uncovered, and top with the cooked bacon. Press the cheese and bacon into the bread lightly to help anchor it to the bread and prevent it from blowing around in the air fryer.
9. Air fry for one or two more minutes, just to melt the cheese and finish cooking the egg. Serve immediately.

Perfect Cinnamon Toast

Servings: 6
Cooking Time: 10 Minutes
Ingredients:
- 12 slices whole-wheat bread
- 1 stick butter, room temperature
- ½ cup white sugar
- 1½ teaspoons ground cinnamon
- 1½ teaspoons pure vanilla extract
- 1 pinch kosher salt
- 2 pinches freshly ground black pepper (optional)

Directions:
1. Mash the softened butter with a fork or the back of a spoon in a bowl. Add the sugar, cinnamon, vanilla, and salt. Stir until everything is well combined.
2. Spread one-sixth of the mixture onto each slice of bread, making sure to cover the entire surface.
3. Install a crisper plate in both drawers. Place half the bread sliced in the zone 1 drawer and half in the zone 2 drawer, then insert the drawers into the unit.
4. Select zone 1, select AIR FRY, set temperature to 400 degrees F/ 200 degrees C, and set time to 5 minutes. Select MATCH to match zone 2 settings to zone 1. Press theSTART/STOP button to begin cooking
5. When cooking is complete, remove the slices and cut them diagonally.
6. Serve immediately.

Nutrition:
- (Per serving) Calories 322 | Fat 16.5g | Sodium 249mg | Carbs 39.3g | Fiber 4.2g | Sugar 18.2g | Protein 8.2g

Cheddar-ham-corn Muffins

Servings: 8 Muffins
Cooking Time: 6 To 8 Minutes
Ingredients:
- 180 ml cornmeal/polenta
- 60 ml flour
- 1½ teaspoons baking powder
- ¼ teaspoon salt
- 1 egg, beaten
- 2 tablespoons rapeseed oil
- 120 ml milk
- 120 ml shredded sharp Cheddar cheese
- 120 ml diced ham
- 8 foil muffin cups, liners removed and sprayed with cooking spray

Directions:
1. Preheat the air fryer to 200°C.
2. In a medium bowl, stir together the cornmeal, flour, baking powder, and salt.
3. Add egg, oil, and milk to dry ingredients and mix well.
4. Stir in shredded cheese and diced ham.
5. Divide batter among the muffin cups.
6. Place filled muffin cups in two air fryer drawers and bake for 5 minutes.
7. Reduce temperature to 166°C and bake for 1 to 2 minutes or until toothpick inserted in center of muffin comes out clean.

Breakfast Stuffed Peppers

Servings: 4
Cooking Time: 13 Minutes
Ingredients:
- 2 capsicums, halved, seeds removed
- 4 eggs
- 1 teaspoon olive oil
- 1 pinch salt and pepper
- 1 pinch sriracha flakes

Directions:
1. Cut each capsicum in half and place two halves in each air fryer basket.
2. Crack one egg into each capsicum and top it with black pepper, salt, sriracha flakes and olive oil.
3. Return the air fryer basket 1 to Zone 1, and basket 2 to Zone 2 of the Ninja Foodi 2-Basket Air Fryer.
4. Choose the "Air Fry" mode for Zone 1 at 390 degrees F and 13 minutes of cooking time.
5. Select the "MATCH COOK" option to copy the settings for Zone 2.
6. Initiate cooking by pressing the START/PAUSE BUTTON.
7. Serve warm.

Nutrition:
- (Per serving) Calories 237 | Fat 19g |Sodium 518mg | Carbs 7g | Fiber 1.5g | Sugar 3.4g | Protein 12g

Breakfast Cheese Sandwich

Servings: 2
Cooking Time: 8 Minutes
Ingredients:
- 4 bread slices
- 2 provolone cheese slice
- ¼ tsp dried basil
- 2 tbsp mayonnaise
- 2 Monterey jack cheese slice
- 2 cheddar cheese slice
- ¼ tsp dried oregano

Directions:
1. In a small bowl, mix mayonnaise, basil, and oregano.
2. Spread mayonnaise on one side of the two bread slices.
3. Top two bread slices with cheddar cheese, provolone cheese, Monterey jack cheese slice, and cover with remaining bread slices.
4. Insert a crisper plate in the Ninja Foodi air fryer baskets.
5. Place sandwiches in both baskets.
6. Select zone 1, then select "air fry" mode and set the temperature to 390 degrees F for 8 minutes. Press "match" to match zone 2 settings to zone 1. Press "start/stop" to begin. Turn halfway through.

Nutrition:
- (Per serving) Calories 421 | Fat 30.7g |Sodium 796mg | Carbs 13.9g | Fiber 0.5g | Sugar 2.2g | Protein 22.5g

Donuts

Servings: 6
Cooking Time: 15 Minutes
Ingredients:
- 1 cup granulated sugar
- 2 tablespoons ground cinnamon
- 1 can refrigerated flaky buttermilk biscuits
- ¼ cup unsalted butter, melted

Directions:
1. Combine the sugar and cinnamon in a small shallow bowl and set aside.
2. Remove the biscuits from the can and put them on a chopping board, separated. Cut holes in the center of each biscuit with a 1-inch round biscuit cutter (or a similarly sized bottle cap).
3. Place a crisper plate in each drawer. In each drawer, place 4 biscuits in a single layer. Insert the drawers into the unit.
4. Select zone 1, then AIR FRY, then set the temperature to 360 degrees F/ 180 degrees C with a 10-minute timer. To match zone 2 settings to zone 1, choose MATCH. To begin cooking, select START/STOP.
5. Remove the donuts from the drawers after the timer has finished.

Nutrition:
- (Per serving) Calories 223 | Fat 8g | Sodium 150mg | Carbs 40g | Fiber 1.4g | Sugar 34.2g | Protein 0.8g

Snacks And Appetizers Recipes

Fried Halloumi Cheese

Servings: 6
Cooking Time: 12 Minutes.
Ingredients:
- 1 block of halloumi cheese, sliced
- 2 teaspoons olive oil

Directions:
1. Divide the halloumi cheese slices in the crisper plate.
2. Drizzle olive oil over the cheese slices.
3. Return the crisper plate to the Ninja Foodi Dual Zone Air Fryer.
4. Choose the Air Fry mode for Zone 1 and set the temperature to 360 degrees F and the time to 12 minutes.
5. Flip the cheese slices once cooked halfway through.
6. Serve.

Nutrition:
- (Per serving) Calories 186 | Fat 3g |Sodium 223mg | Carbs 31g | Fiber 8.7g | Sugar 5.5g | Protein 9.7g

Mozzarella Arancini

Servings: 16 Arancini
Cooking Time: 8 To 11 Minutes
Ingredients:
- 475 ml cooked rice, cooled
- 2 eggs, beaten
- 355 ml panko breadcrumbs, divided
- 120 ml grated Parmesan cheese
- 2 tablespoons minced fresh basil
- 16 ¾-inch cubes Mozzarella cheese
- 2 tablespoons olive oil

Directions:
1. Preheat the air fryer to 205°C.
2. In a medium bowl, combine the rice, eggs, 120 ml of the breadcrumbs, Parmesan cheese, and basil. Form this mixture into 16 1½-inch balls.
3. Poke a hole in each of the balls with your finger and insert a Mozzarella cube. Form the rice mixture firmly around the cheese.
4. On a shallow plate, combine the remaining 240 ml of the breadcrumbs with the olive oil and mix well. Roll the rice balls in the breadcrumbs to coat.
5. Air fry the arancini in two baskets for 8 to 11 minutes or until golden brown.
6. Serve hot.

Sweet Bites

Servings: 4
Cooking Time: 12
Ingredients:
- 10 sheets of Phyllo dough, (filo dough)
- 2 tablespoons of melted butter
- 1 cup walnuts, chopped
- 2 teaspoons of honey
- Pinch of cinnamon
- 1 teaspoon of orange zest

Directions:
1. First, layer together 10 Phyllo dough sheets on a flat surface.
2. Then cut it into 4 *4-inch squares.
3. Now, coat the squares with butter, drizzle some honey, orange zest, walnuts, and cinnamon.
4. Bring all 4 corners together and press the corners to make a little like purse design.
5. Divide it amongst air fryer basket and select zone 1 basket using AIR fry mode and set it for 7 minutes at 375 degrees F.
6. Select the MATCH button for the zone 2 basket.
7. Once done, take out and serve.

Nutrition:
- (Per serving) Calories 397| Fat 27.1 g| Sodium 271mg | Carbs31.2 g | Fiber 3.2g| Sugar3.3g | Protein 11g

Goat Cheese And Garlic Crostini & Sweet Bacon Potato Crunchies

Servings: 8
Cooking Time: 7 Minutes
Ingredients:
- Goat Cheese and Garlic Crostini:
- 1 wholemeal baguette
- 60 ml olive oil
- 2 garlic cloves, minced
- 113 g goat cheese
- 2 tablespoons fresh basil, minced
- Sweet Bacon Potato Crunchies:
- 24 frozen potato crunchies
- 6 slices cooked bacon
- 2 tablespoons maple syrup
- 240 ml shredded Cheddar cheese

Directions:
1. Make the Goat Cheese and Garlic Crostini :
2. Preheat the air fryer to 190°C.
3. Cut the baguette into ½-inch-thick slices.
4. In a small bowl, mix together the olive oil and garlic, then brush it over one side of each slice of bread.
5. Place the olive-oil-coated bread in a single layer in the zone 1 air fryer basket and bake for 5 minutes.
6. Meanwhile, in a small bowl, mix together the goat cheese and basil.
7. Remove the toast from the air fryer, then spread a thin layer of the goat cheese mixture over the top of each piece and serve.
8. Make the Sweet Bacon Potato Crunchies :
9. Preheat the air fryer to 205°C.
10. Put the potato crunchies in the zone 2 air fryer basket. Air fry for 10 minutes, shaking the basket halfway through the cooking time.
11. Meanwhile, cut the bacon into 1-inch pieces.
12. Remove the potato crunchies from the air fryer basket and put into a baking pan. Top with the bacon and drizzle with the maple syrup. Air fry for 5 minutes, or until the crunchies and bacon are crisp.
13. Top with the cheese and air fry for 2 minutes, or until the cheese is melted.
14. Serve hot.

Ravioli

Servings: 2
Cooking Time: 6 Minutes
Ingredients:
- 12 frozen portions of ravioli
- ½ cup buttermilk
- ½ cup Italian breadcrumbs

Directions:
1. Place two bowls side by side. Put the buttermilk in one and breadcrumbs in the other.
2. Dip each piece of ravioli into the buttermilk then breadcrumbs, making sure to coat them as best as possible.
3. Place a crisper plate in both drawers. In each drawer, put four breaded ravioli pieces in a single layer. Insert the drawers into the unit.
4. Select zone 1, then AIR FRY, then set the temperature to 360 degrees F/ 180 degrees C with a 6-minute timer. To match zone 2 settings to zone 1, choose MATCH. To begin, select START/STOP.
5. Remove the ravioli from the drawers after the timer has finished.

Nutrition:
- (Per serving) Calories 481 | Fat 20g | Sodium 1162mg | Carbs 56g | Fiber 4g | Sugar 9g | Protein 19g

Onion Rings

Servings: 4
Cooking Time: 10 Minutes
Ingredients:
- 170g onion, sliced into rings
- ½ cup breadcrumbs
- 2 eggs, beaten
- ½ cup flour
- Salt and black pepper to taste

Directions:
1. Mix flour, black pepper and salt in a bowl.
2. Dredge the onion rings through the flour mixture.
3. Dip them in the eggs and coat with the breadcrumbs.
4. Place the coated onion rings in the air fryer baskets.
5. Return the air fryer basket 1 to Zone 1, and basket 2 to Zone 2 of the Ninja Foodi 2-Basket Air Fryer.
6. Choose the "Air Fry" mode for Zone 1 at 350 degrees F and 7 minutes of cooking time.
7. Select the "MATCH COOK" option to copy the settings for Zone 2.
8. Initiate cooking by pressing the START/PAUSE BUTTON.
9. Shake the rings once cooked halfway through.
10. Serve warm.

Beef Taquitos

Servings: 8
Cooking Time: 6 Minutes
Ingredients:
- 455g lean beef mince
- 1 teaspoon salt
- 70g salsa
- ½ teaspoon granulated garlic
- ½ teaspoon chili powder
- ½ teaspoon cumin
- 100g shredded cheese
- 12 mini corn tortillas

Directions:
1. Season beef mince with salt in a frying pan and cook over medium-high heat.
2. Cook until the meat is nicely browned, stirring frequently and breaking it into fine crumbles. Remove from the heat and drain any remaining grease.
3. Stir in the salsa, garlic, chili powder, cumin, and cheese until all ingredients are completely incorporated, and the cheese has melted.
4. Warm tortillas on a grill or iron frying pan to make them flexible. Allow them to warm rather than crisp and brown.
5. Fill each tortilla with about 1 to 2 tablespoons of the meat mixture and roll it up.
6. Press either "Zone 1" or "Zone 2" and then rotate the knob to select "Air Fryer".
7. Set the temperature to 175 degrees C, and then set the time for 5 minutes to preheat.
8. After preheating, arrange them into the basket.
9. Slide the basket into the Air Fryer and set the time for 6 minutes.
10. After cooking time is completed, place on a wire rack for a few minutes, then transfer onto serving plates and serve.

Potato Tater Tots

Servings: 4
Cooking Time: 27 Minutes.

Ingredients:
- 2 potatoes, peeled
- ½ teaspoon Cajun seasoning
- Olive oil cooking spray
- Sea salt to taste

Directions:
1. Boil water in a cooking pot and cook potatoes in it for 15 minutes.
2. Drain and leave the potatoes to cool in a bowl.
3. Grate these potatoes and toss them with Cajun seasoning.
4. Make small tater tots out of this mixture.
5. Divide them into the two crisper plates and spray them with cooking oil.
6. Return the crisper plates to the Ninja Foodi Dual Zone Air Fryer.
7. Choose the Air Fry mode for Zone 1 and set the temperature to 375 degrees F and the time to 27 minutes.
8. Select the "MATCH" button to copy the settings for Zone 2.
9. Initiate cooking by pressing the START/STOP button.
10. Flip them once cooked halfway through, and resume cooking.
11. Serve warm

Nutrition:
- (Per serving) Calories 185 | Fat 11g | Sodium 355mg | Carbs 21g | Fiber 5.8g | Sugar 3g | Protein 4.7g

Kale Chips

Servings: 4
Cooking Time: 3 Minutes

Ingredients:
- 1 head fresh kale, stems and ribs removed and cut into 4cm pieces
- 1 tablespoon olive oil
- 1 teaspoon soy sauce
- ⅛ teaspoon cayenne pepper
- Pinch of freshly ground black pepper

Directions:
1. In a large bowl, add all the ingredients and mix well.
2. Grease basket of Ninja Foodi 2-Basket Air Fryer.
3. Press your chosen zone - "Zone 1" or "Zone 2" and then rotate the knob to select "Air Fry".
4. Set the temperature to 200 degrees C and then set the time for 5 minutes to preheat.
5. After preheating, arrange the kale pieces into the basket of each zone.
6. Slide the basket into the Air Fryer and set the time for 3 minutes.
7. While cooking, toss the kale pieces once halfway through.
8. After cooking time is completed, remove the kale chips and baking pans from Air Fryer.
9. Place the kale chips onto a wire rack to cool for about 10 minutes before serving.

Spicy Chicken Tenders

Servings: 2
Cooking Time: 12

Ingredients:
- 2 large eggs, whisked
- 2 tablespoons lemon juice
- Salt and black pepper
- 1 pound of chicken tenders
- 1 cup Panko breadcrumbs
- 1/2 cup Italian bread crumb
- 1 teaspoon smoked paprika
- 1/4 teaspoon garlic powder
- 1/4 teaspoon onion powder
- 1/2 cup fresh grated parmesan cheese

Directions:
1. Take a bowl and whisk eggs in it and set aside for further use.
2. In a large bowl add lemon juice, paprika, salt, black pepper, garlic powder, onion powder
3. In a separate bowl mix Panko breadcrumbs, Italian bread crumbs, and parmesan cheese.
4. Dip the chicken tender in the spice mixture and coat the entire tender well.
5. Let the tenders sit for 1 hour.
6. Then dip each chicken tender in egg and then in bread crumbs.
7. Line both the basket of the air fryer with parchment paper.
8. Divide the tenders between the baskets.
9. Set zone 1 basket to air fry mode at 350 degrees F for 12 minutes.
10. Select the MATCH button for the zone 2 basket.
11. Once it's done, serve.

Nutrition:
- (Per serving) Calories 836| Fat 36g| Sodium 1307 mg | Carbs 31.3g | Fiber 2.5g| Sugar 3.3 g | Protein 95.3g

Miso-glazed Shishito Peppers Charred Lemon Shishito Peppers

Servings: 4
Cooking Time: 10 Minutes

Ingredients:
- FOR THE MISO-GLAZED PEPPERS
- 2 tablespoons vegetable oil
- 2 tablespoons water
- 1 tablespoon white miso
- 1 teaspoon grated fresh ginger
- ½ pound shishito peppers
- FOR THE CHARRED LEMON PEPPERS
- ½ pound shishito peppers
- 1 lemon, cut into ⅛-inch-thick rounds
- 2 garlic cloves, minced
- 2 tablespoons vegetable oil
- ½ teaspoon kosher salt

Directions:

1. To prep the miso-glazed peppers: In a large bowl, mix the vegetable oil, water, miso, and ginger until well combined. Add the shishitos and toss to coat.

2. To prep the charred lemon peppers: In a large bowl, combine the shishitos, lemon slices, garlic, vegetable oil, and salt. Toss to coat.

3. To cook the peppers: Install a crisper plate in each of the two baskets. Place the miso-glazed peppers in the Zone 1 basket and insert the basket in the unit. Place the peppers with lemons in the Zone 2 basket and insert the basket in the unit.

4. Select Zone 1, select AIR FRY, set the temperature to 390°F, and set the time to 10 minutes. Select MATCH COOK to match Zone 2 settings to Zone 1.

5. Press START/PAUSE to begin cooking.

6. When both timers read 4 minutes, press START/PAUSE. Remove both baskets and shake well. Reinsert the baskets and press START/PAUSE to resume cooking.

7. When cooking is complete, serve immediately.

Nutrition:
- (Per serving) Calories: 165; Total fat: 14g; Saturated fat: 2g; Carbohydrates: 9g; Fiber: 2g; Protein: 2g; Sodium: 334mg

Beef Jerky Pineapple Jerky

Servings: 8
Cooking Time: 6 To 12 Hours

Ingredients:
- FOR THE BEEF JERKY
- ½ cup reduced-sodium soy sauce
- ¼ cup pineapple juice
- 1 tablespoon dark brown sugar
- 1 tablespoon Worcestershire sauce
- ½ teaspoon smoked paprika
- ¼ teaspoon freshly ground black pepper
- ¼ teaspoon red pepper flakes
- 1 pound beef bottom round, trimmed of excess fat, cut into ¼-inch-thick slices
- FOR THE PINEAPPLE JERKY
- 1 pound pineapple, cut into ⅛-inch-thick rounds, pat dry
- 1 teaspoon chili powder (optional)

Directions:

1. To prep the beef jerky: In a large zip-top bag, combine the soy sauce, pineapple juice, brown sugar, Worcestershire sauce, smoked paprika, black pepper, and red pepper flakes.

2. Add the beef slices, seal the bag, and toss to coat the meat in the marinade. Refrigerate overnight or for at least 8 hours.

3. Remove the beef slices and discard the marinade. Using a paper towel, pat the slices dry to remove excess marinade.

4. To prep the pineapple jerky: Sprinkle the pineapple with chili powder (if using).

5. To dehydrate the jerky: Arrange half of the beef slices in a single layer in the Zone 1 basket, making sure they do not overlap. Place a crisper plate on top of the beef slices and arrange the remaining slices in a single layer on top of the crisper plate. Insert the basket in the unit.

6. Repeat this process with the pineapple in the Zone 2 basket and insert the basket in the unit.

7. Select Zone 1, select DEHYDRATE, set the temperature to 150°F, and set the time to 8 hours.

8. Select Zone 2, select DEHYDRATE, set the temperature to 135°F, and set the time to 12 hours.

9. Press START/PAUSE to begin cooking.

10. When the Zone 1 timer reads 2 hours, press START/PAUSE. Remove the basket and check the beef jerky for doneness. If necessary, reinsert the basket and press START/PAUSE to resume cooking.

Nutrition:
- (Per serving) Calories: 171; Total fat: 6.5g; Saturated fat: 2g; Carbohydrates: 2g; Fiber: 0g; Protein: 25g; Sodium: 369mg

Lemony Pear Chips

Servings: 4
Cooking Time: 9 To 13 Minutes
Ingredients:
- 2 firm Bosc or Anjou pears, cut crosswise into ⅛-inch-thick slices
- 1 tablespoon freshly squeezed lemon juice
- ½ teaspoon ground cinnamon
- ⅛ teaspoon ground cardamom

Directions:
1. Preheat the air fryer to 190°C.
2. Separate the smaller stem-end pear rounds from the larger rounds with seeds. Remove the core and seeds from the larger slices. Sprinkle all slices with lemon juice, cinnamon, and cardamom.
3. Put the chips into the two air fryer baskets. Air fry for 5 to 8 minutes, or until light golden brown, shaking the baskets once during cooking. Remove from the air fryer.
4. Remove the chips from the air fryer. Cool and serve or store in an airtight container at room temperature up for to 2 days.

Mozzarella Balls

Servings: 6
Cooking Time: 15 Minutes
Ingredients:
- 2 cups mozzarella, shredded
- 3 tablespoons cornstarch
- 3 tablespoons water
- 2 eggs, beaten
- 1 cup Italian seasoned breadcrumbs
- 1 tablespoon Italian seasoning
- 1½ teaspoons garlic powder
- 1 teaspoon salt
- 1½ teaspoons Parmesan

Directions:
1. Mix mozzarella with parmesan, water and cornstarch in a bowl.
2. Make 1-inch balls out of this mixture.
3. Mix breadcrumbs with seasoning, salt, and garlic powder in a bowl.
4. Dip the balls into the beaten eggs and coat with the breadcrumbs.
5. Place the coated balls in the air fryer baskets.
6. Return the air fryer basket 1 to Zone 1, and basket 2 to Zone 2 of the Ninja Foodi 2-Basket Air Fryer.
7. Choose the "Air Fry" mode for Zone 1 and set the temperature to 360 degrees F and 13 minutes of cooking time.
8. Select the "MATCH COOK" option to copy the settings for Zone 2.
9. Initiate cooking by pressing the START/PAUSE BUTTON.
10. Toss the balls once cooked halfway through.
11. Serve.

Crispy Calamari Rings

Servings: 4
Cooking Time: 10 Minutes
Ingredients:
- 455g calamari rings, patted dry
- 3 tablespoons lemon juice
- 60g plain flour
- 1 teaspoon garlic powder
- 2 egg whites
- 60ml milk
- 220g panko breadcrumbs
- 1½ teaspoon salt
- 1½ teaspoon ground black pepper

Directions:
1. Allow the squid rings to marinade for at least 30 minutes in a bowl with lemon juice. Drain the water in a colander.
2. In a shallow bowl, combine the flour and garlic powder.
3. In a separate bowl, whisk together the egg whites and milk.
4. In a third bowl, combine the panko breadcrumbs, salt, and pepper.
5. Floured first the calamari rings, then dip in the egg mixture, and finally in the panko breadcrumb mixture.
6. Press either "Zone 1" or "Zone 2" and then rotate the knob to select "Air Fry".
7. Set the temperature to 200 degrees C, and then set the time for 5 minutes to preheat.
8. After preheating, spray the Air-Fryer basket with cooking spray and line with parchment paper. Arrange in a single layer and spritz them with cooking spray.
9. Slide the basket into the Air Fryer and set the time for 10 minutes.
10. After cooking time is completed, transfer them onto serving plates and serve.

Sausage Balls With Cheese

Servings: 8
Cooking Time: 10 To 11 Minutes
Ingredients:
- 340 g mild sausage meat
- 355 ml baking mix
- 240 ml shredded mild Cheddar cheese
- 85 g soft white cheese, at room temperature
- 1 to 2 tablespoons olive oil

Directions:
1. Preheat the air fryer to 165°C. Line the two air fryer baskets with parchment paper.
2. Mix together the ground sausage, baking mix, Cheddar cheese, and soft white cheese in a large bowl and stir to incorporate.
3. Divide the sausage mixture into 16 equal portions and roll them into 1-inch balls with your hands.
4. Arrange the sausage balls on the parchment, leaving space between each ball.
5. Brush the sausage balls with the olive oil. Bake in the two baskets for 10 to 11 minutes, shaking the baskets halfway through, or until the balls are firm and lightly browned on both sides.
6. Remove from the baskets to a plate.
7. Serve warm.

Chicken Tenders

Servings:3
Cooking Time:12
Ingredients:
- 1 pound of chicken tender
- Salt and black pepper, to taste
- 1 cup Panko bread crumbs
- 2 cups Italian bread crumbs
- 1 cup parmesan cheese
- 2 eggs
- Oil spray, for greasing

Directions:
1. Sprinkle the tenders with salt and black pepper.
2. In a medium bowl mix Panko bread crumbs with Italian breadcrumbs.
3. Add salt, pepper, and parmesan cheese.
4. Crack two eggs in a bowl.
5. First, put the chicken tender in eggs.
6. Now dredge the tender in a bowl and coat the tender well with crumbs.
7. Line both of the baskets of the air fryer with parchment paper.
8. At the end spray the tenders with oil spray.
9. Divided the tenders between the baskets of Ninja Foodie 2-Basket Air Fryer.
10. Set zone 1 basket to AIR FRY mode at 350 degrees F for 12 minutes.
11. Select the MATCH button for the zone 2 basket.
12. Once it's done, serve.

Nutrition:
- (Per serving) Calories558 | Fat23.8g | Sodium872 mg | Carbs 20.9g | Fiber1.7 g| Sugar2.2 g | Protein 63.5g

Beef Skewers

Servings: 6
Cooking Time: 5 Minutes
Ingredients:
- 1 beef flank steak
- 240ml rice vinegar
- 240ml soy sauce
- 55g packed brown sugar
- 2 tablespoons minced fresh gingerroot
- 6 garlic cloves, minced
- 3 teaspoons sesame oil
- 1 teaspoon hot pepper sauce
- ½ teaspoon cornflour

Directions:
1. Cut beef into ½ cm thick strips. Whisk together the following 7 ingredients in a large mixing bowl until well combined.
2. In a shallow dish, pour 1 cup of marinade. Toss in the beef and turn to coat. Refrigerate for 2-8 hours, covered. Cover and keep the remaining marinade refrigerated.
3. Beef should be drained. 12 metal or wet wooden skewers threaded with beef.
4. Press either "Zone 1" or "Zone 2" and then rotate the knob to select "Air Fry".
5. Set the temperature to 200 degrees C, and then set the time for 5 minutes to preheat.
6. After preheating, spray the basket with cooking spray and arrange skewers onto basket.
7. Slide the basket into the Air Fryer and set the time for 5 minutes.
8. After cooking time is completed, transfer them onto serving plates and serve.

Cinnamon Sugar Chickpeas

Servings: 4
Cooking Time: 15 Minutes
Ingredients:
- 2 cups chickpeas, drained
- Spray oil
- 1 tablespoon coconut sugar
- ½ teaspoon cinnamon
- Serving
- 57g cheddar cheese, cubed
- ¼ cup raw almonds
- 85g jerky, sliced

Directions:
1. Toss chickpeas with coconut sugar, cinnamon and oil in a bowl.
2. Divide the chickpeas into the Ninja Foodi 2 Baskets Air Fryer baskets.
3. Drizzle cheddar cheese, almonds and jerky on top.
4. Return the air fryer basket 1 to Zone 1, and basket 2 to Zone 2 of the Ninja Foodi 2-Basket Air Fryer.
5. Choose the "Air Fry" mode for Zone 1 at 380 degrees F and 15 minutes of cooking time.
6. Select the "MATCH COOK" option to copy the settings for Zone 2.
7. Initiate cooking by pressing the START/PAUSE BUTTON.
8. Toss the chickpeas once cooked halfway through.
9. Serve warm.

Crab Cakes

Servings: 4
Cooking Time: 15 Minutes
Ingredients:
- 227g lump crab meat
- 1 red capsicum, chopped
- 3 green onions, chopped
- 3 tablespoons mayonnaise
- 3 tablespoons breadcrumbs
- 2 teaspoons old bay seasoning
- 1 teaspoon lemon juice

Directions:
1. Mix crab meat with capsicum, onions and the rest of the ingredients in a food processor.
2. Make 4 inch crab cakes out of this mixture.
3. Divide the crab cakes into the Ninja Foodi 2 Baskets Air Fryer baskets.
4. Return the air fryer basket 1 to Zone 1, and basket 2 to Zone 2 of the Ninja Foodi 2-Basket Air Fryer.
5. Choose the "Air Fry" mode for Zone 1 at 370 degrees F and 10 minutes of cooking time.
6. Select the "MATCH COOK" option to copy the settings for Zone 2.
7. Initiate cooking by pressing the START/PAUSE BUTTON.
8. Flip the crab cakes once cooked halfway through.
9. Serve warm.

Crispy Tortilla Chips

Servings: 8
Cooking Time: 13 Minutes.
Ingredients:
- 4 (6-inch) corn tortillas
- 1 tablespoon Avocado Oil
- Sea salt to taste
- Cooking spray

Directions:
1. Spread the corn tortillas on the working surface.
2. Slice them into bite-sized triangles.
3. Toss them with salt and cooking oil.
4. Divide the triangles in the two crisper plates into a single layer.
5. Return the crisper plates to the Ninja Foodi Dual Zone Air Fryer.
6. Choose the Air Fry mode for Zone 1 and set the temperature to 390 degrees F and the time to 13 minutes.
7. Select the "MATCH" button to copy the settings for Zone 2.
8. Initiate cooking by pressing the START/STOP button.
9. Toss the chips once cooked halfway through, then resume cooking.
10. Serve and enjoy.

Nutrition:
- (Per serving) Calories 103 | Fat 8.4g |Sodium 117mg | Carbs 3.5g | Fiber 0.9g | Sugar 1.5g | Protein 5.1g

Cottage Fries

Servings: 2
Cooking Time: 12 Minutes
Ingredients:
- 3 medium russet potatoes, sliced
- 1 teaspoon olive oil
- Salt and pepper, to taste

Directions:
1. Potatoes should be washed and dried. Cut them into ½ cm slices.
2. Soak the slices in cold water for 3 minutes to remove the starch.
3. Remove the potatoes from the water and pat them dry. Toss them in a bowl with olive oil, pepper and a pinch of salt.
4. Press either "Zone 1" or "Zone 2" and then rotate the knob to select "Air Fryer".
5. Set the temperature to 200 degrees C, and then set the time for 5 minutes to preheat.
6. After preheating, arrange potatoes into the basket.
7. Slide the basket into the Air Fryer and set the time for 12 minutes.
8. While cooking, toss the potato pieces once halfway through.
9. After cooking time is completed, transfer the fries onto serving plates and serve.

Vegetables And Sides Recipes

Balsamic-glazed Tofu With Roasted Butternut Squash

Servings: 4
Cooking Time: 40 Minutes
Ingredients:
- FOR THE BALSAMIC TOFU
- 2 tablespoons balsamic vinegar
- 1 tablespoon maple syrup
- 1 teaspoon soy sauce
- 1 teaspoon Dijon mustard
- 1 (14-ounce) package firm tofu, drained and cut into large cubes
- 1 tablespoon canola oil
- FOR THE BUTTERNUT SQUASH
- 1 small butternut squash
- 1 tablespoon canola oil
- 1 teaspoon light brown sugar
- ¼ teaspoon kosher salt
- ¼ teaspoon freshly ground black pepper

Directions:
1. To prep the balsamic tofu: In a large bowl, whisk together the vinegar, maple syrup, soy sauce, and mustard. Add the tofu and stir to coat. Cover and marinate for at least 20 minutes (or up to overnight in the refrigerator).
2. To prep the butternut squash: Peel the squash and cut in half lengthwise. Remove and discard the seeds. Cut the squash crosswise into ½-inch-thick slices.
3. Brush the squash pieces with the oil, then sprinkle with the brown sugar, salt, and black pepper.
4. To cook the tofu and squash: Install a crisper plate in each of the two baskets. Place the tofu in the Zone 1 basket, drizzle with the oil, and insert the basket in the unit. Place the squash in the Zone 2 basket and insert the basket in the unit.
5. Select Zone 1, select AIR FRY, set the temperature to 400°F, and set the timer to 10 minutes.
6. Select Zone 2, select ROAST, set the temperature to 400°F, and set the timer to 40 minutes. Select SMART FINISH.
7. Press START/PAUSE to begin cooking.
8. When cooking is complete, the tofu will have begun to crisp and brown around the edges and the squash should be tender. Serve hot.

Nutrition:
- (Per serving) Calories: 253; Total fat: 11g; Saturated fat: 1g; Carbohydrates: 30g; Fiber: 4.5g; Protein: 11g; Sodium: 237mg

Fried Avocado Tacos

Servings: 4
Cooking Time: 10 Minutes
Ingredients:
- For the sauce:
- 2 cups shredded fresh kale or coleslaw mix
- ¼ cup minced fresh cilantro
- ¼ cup plain Greek yogurt
- 2 tablespoons lime juice
- 1 teaspoon honey
- ¼ teaspoon salt
- ¼ teaspoon ground chipotle pepper
- ¼ teaspoon pepper
- For the tacos:
- 1 large egg, beaten
- ¼ cup cornmeal
- ½ teaspoon salt
- ½ teaspoon garlic powder
- ½ teaspoon ground chipotle pepper
- 2 medium avocados, peeled and sliced
- Cooking spray
- 8 flour tortillas or corn tortillas (6 inches), heated up
- 1 medium tomato, chopped
- Crumbled queso fresco (optional)

Directions:
1. Combine the first 8 ingredients in a bowl. Cover and refrigerate until serving.
2. Place the egg in a shallow bowl. In another shallow bowl, mix the cornmeal, salt, garlic powder, and chipotle pepper.
3. Dip the avocado slices in the egg, then into the cornmeal mixture, gently patting to help adhere.
4. Place a crisper plate in both drawers. Put the avocado slices in the drawers in a single layer. Insert the drawers into the unit.
5. Select zone 1, then AIR FRY, then set the temperature to 360 degrees F/ 180 degrees C with a 6-minute timer. To match zone 2 settings to zone 1, choose MATCH. To begin, select START/STOP.
6. Put the avocado slices, prepared sauce, tomato, and queso fresco in the tortillas and serve.

Garlic-rosemary Brussels Sprouts

Servings: 4
Cooking Time: 15 Minutes
Ingredients:
- 3 tablespoons olive oil
- 2 garlic cloves, minced
- ½ teaspoon salt
- ¼ teaspoon pepper
- 1-pound Brussels sprouts, trimmed and halved
- ½ cup panko breadcrumbs
- 1½ teaspoons minced fresh rosemary

Directions:
1. Place the first 4 ingredients in a small microwave-safe bowl| microwave on high for 30 seconds.
2. Toss the Brussels sprouts in 2 tablespoons of the microwaved mixture.
3. Place a crisper plate in each drawer. Put the sprouts in a single layer in each drawer. Insert the drawers into the units.
4. Select zone 1, then AIR FRY, then set the temperature to 360 degrees F/ 180 degrees C with a 6-minute timer. To match zone 2 settings to zone 1, choose MATCH. To begin, select START/STOP.
5. Remove the sprouts from the drawers after the timer has finished.
6. Toss the breadcrumbs with the rosemary and remaining oil mixture| sprinkle over the sprouts.
7. Continue cooking until the crumbs are browned, and the sprouts are tender . Serve immediately.

Mixed Air Fry Veggies

Servings: 4
Cooking Time: 25 Minutes
Ingredients:
- 2 cups carrots, cubed
- 2 cups potatoes, cubed
- 2 cups shallots, cubed
- 2 cups zucchini, diced
- 2 cups yellow squash, cubed
- Salt and black pepper, to taste
- 1 tablespoon Italian seasoning
- 2 tablespoons ranch seasoning
- 4 tablespoons olive oil

Directions:
1. Take a large bowl and add all the veggies to it.
2. Season the veggies with salt, pepper, Italian seasoning, ranch seasoning, and olive oil.
3. Toss all the ingredients well.
4. Divide the veggies into both the baskets of the air fryer.
5. Set zone 1 basket to AIR FRY mode at 360 degrees F for 25 minutes.
6. Select the MATCH button for the zone 2 basket.
7. Once it is cooked and done, serve, and enjoy.

Sweet Potatoes & Brussels Sprouts

Servings: 8
Cooking Time: 35 Minutes
Ingredients:
- 340g sweet potatoes, cubed
- 30ml olive oil
- 150g onion, cut into pieces
- 352g Brussels sprouts, halved
- Pepper
- Salt
- For glaze:
- 78ml ketchup
- 115ml balsamic vinegar
- 15g mustard
- 29 ml honey

Directions:
1. In a bowl, toss Brussels sprouts, oil, onion, sweet potatoes, pepper, and salt.
2. Insert a crisper plate in the Ninja Foodi air fryer baskets.
3. Add Brussels sprouts and sweet potato mixture in both baskets.
4. Select zone 1, then select "air fry" mode and set the temperature to 390 degrees F for 25 minutes. Press "match" to match zone 2 settings to zone 1. Press "start/stop" to begin. Stir halfway through.
5. Meanwhile, add vinegar, ketchup, honey, and mustard to a saucepan and cook over medium heat for 5-10 minutes.
6. Toss cooked sweet potatoes and Brussels sprouts with sauce.

Nutrition:
- (Per serving) Calories 142 | Fat 4.2g |Sodium 147mg | Carbs 25.2g | Fiber 4g | Sugar 8.8g | Protein 2.9g

Zucchini With Stuffing

Servings: 3
Cooking Time: 20
Ingredients:
- 1 cup quinoa, rinsed
- 1 cup black olives
- 6 medium zucchinis, about 2 pounds
- 2 cups cannellini beans, drained
- 1 white onion, chopped
- ¼ cup almonds, chopped
- 4 cloves of garlic, chopped
- 4 tablespoons olive oil
- 1 cup of water
- 2 cups Parmesan cheese, for topping

Directions:
1. First wash the zucchini and cut it lengthwise.
2. Take a skillet and heat oil in it
3. Sauté the onion in olive oil for a few minutes.
4. Then add the quinoa and water and let it cook for 8 minutes with the lid on the top.
5. Transfer the quinoa to a bowl and add all remaining ingredients excluding zucchini and Parmesan cheese.
6. Scoop out the seeds of zucchinis.
7. Fill the cavity of zucchinis with bowl mixture.
8. Top it with a handful of Parmesan cheese.
9. Arrange 4 zucchinis in both air fryer baskets.
10. Select zone1 basket at AIR FRY for 20 minutes and adjusting the temperature to 390 degrees F.
11. Use the Match button to select the same setting for zone 2.
12. Serve and enjoy.

Nutrition:
- (Per serving) Calories 1171| Fat 48.6g| Sodium 1747mg | Carbs 132.4g | Fiber 42.1g | Sugar 11.5g | Protein 65.7g

Potatoes & Beans

Servings: 4
Cooking Time: 25 Minutes
Ingredients:
- 453g potatoes, cut into pieces
- 15ml olive oil
- 1 tsp garlic powder
- 160g green beans, trimmed
- Pepper
- Salt

Directions:
1. In a bowl, toss green beans, garlic powder, potatoes, oil, pepper, and salt.
2. Insert a crisper plate in the Ninja Foodi air fryer baskets.
3. Add green beans and potato mixture to both baskets.
4. Select zone 1 then select "air fry" mode and set the temperature to 380 degrees F for 25 minutes. Press "match" to match zone 2 settings to zone 1. Press "start/stop" to begin. Stir halfway through.

Nutrition:
- (Per serving) Calories 128 | Fat 3.7g |Sodium 49mg | Carbs 22.4g | Fiber 4.7g | Sugar 2.3g | Protein 3.1g

Buffalo Seitan With Crispy Zucchini Noodles

Servings: 4
Cooking Time: 12 Minutes

Ingredients:
- FOR THE BUFFALO SEITAN
- 1 (8-ounce) package precooked seitan strips
- 1 teaspoon garlic powder, divided
- ½ teaspoon onion powder
- ¼ teaspoon smoked paprika
- ¼ cup Louisiana-style hot sauce
- 2 tablespoons vegetable oil
- 1 tablespoon tomato paste
- ¼ teaspoon freshly ground black pepper
- FOR THE ZUCCHINI NOODLES
- 3 large egg whites
- 1¼ cups all-purpose flour
- 1 teaspoon kosher salt, divided
- 12 ounces seltzer water or club soda
- 5 ounces zucchini noodles
- Nonstick cooking spray

Directions:

1. To prep the Buffalo seitan: Season the seitan strips with ½ teaspoon of garlic powder, the onion powder, and smoked paprika.
2. In a large bowl, whisk together the hot sauce, oil, tomato paste, remaining ½ teaspoon of garlic powder, and the black pepper. Set the bowl of Buffalo sauce aside.
3. To prep the zucchini noodles: In a medium bowl, use a handheld mixer to beat the egg whites until stiff peaks form.
4. In a large bowl, combine the flour and ½ teaspoon of salt. Mix in the seltzer to form a thin batter. Fold in the beaten egg whites.
5. Add the zucchini to the batter and gently mix to coat.
6. To cook the seitan and zucchini noodles: Install a crisper plate in each of the two baskets. Place the seitan in the Zone 1 basket and insert the basket in the unit. Lift the noodles from the batter one at a time, letting the excess drip off, and place them in the Zone 2 basket. Insert the basket in the unit.
7. Select Zone 1, select BAKE, set the temperature to 370°F, and set the timer to 12 minutes.
8. Select Zone 2, select AIR FRY, set the temperature to 400°F, and set the timer to 12 minutes. Select SMART FINISH.
9. Press START/PAUSE to begin cooking.
10. When the Zone 1 timer reads 2 minutes, press START/PAUSE. Remove the basket and transfer the seitan to the bowl of Buffalo sauce. Turn to coat, then return the seitan to the basket. Reinsert the basket and press START/PAUSE to resume cooking.
11. When cooking is complete, the seitan should be warmed through and the zucchini noodles crisp and light golden brown.
12. Sprinkle the zucchini noodles with the remaining ½ teaspoon of salt. If desired, drizzle extra Buffalo sauce over the seitan. Serve hot.

Nutrition:
- (Per serving) Calories: 252; Total fat: 15g; Saturated fat: 1g; Carbohydrates: 22g; Fiber: 1.5g; Protein: 13g; Sodium: 740mg

Breaded Summer Squash

Servings: 4
Cooking Time: 10 Minutes

Ingredients:
- 4 cups yellow summer squash, sliced
- 3 tablespoons olive oil
- ½ teaspoon salt
- ½ teaspoon pepper
- ⅛ teaspoon cayenne pepper
- ¾ cup panko bread crumbs
- ¾ cup grated Parmesan cheese

Directions:

1. Mix crumbs, cheese, cayenne pepper, black pepper, salt and oil in a bowl.
2. Coat the squash slices with the breadcrumb mixture.
3. Place these slices in the air fryer baskets.
4. Return the air fryer basket 1 to Zone 1, and basket 2 to Zone 2 of the Ninja Foodi 2-Basket Air Fryer.
5. Choose the "Air Fry" mode for Zone 1 at 350 degrees F and 10 minutes of cooking time.
6. Select the "MATCH COOK" option to copy the settings for Zone 2.
7. Initiate cooking by pressing the START/PAUSE BUTTON.
8. Flip the squash slices once cooked half way through.
9. Serve warm.

Nutrition:
- (Per serving) Calories 193 | Fat 1g | Sodium 395mg | Carbs 38.7g | Fiber 1.6g | Sugar 0.9g | Protein 6.6g

Quinoa Patties

Servings: 4
Cooking Time: 32 Minutes
Ingredients:
- 1 cup quinoa red
- 1½ cups water
- 1 teaspoon salt
- black pepper, ground
- 1½ cups rolled oats
- 3 eggs beaten
- ¼ cup minced white onion
- ½ cup crumbled feta cheese
- ¼ cup chopped fresh chives
- Salt and black pepper, to taste
- Vegetable or canola oil
- 4 hamburger buns
- 4 arugulas
- 4 slices tomato sliced
- Cucumber yogurt dill sauce
- 1 cup cucumber, diced
- 1 cup Greek yogurt
- 2 teaspoons lemon juice
- ¼ teaspoon salt
- Black pepper, ground
- 1 tablespoon chopped fresh dill
- 1 tablespoon olive oil

Directions:
1. Add quinoa to a saucepan filled with cold water, salt, and black pepper, and place it over medium-high heat.
2. Cook the quinoa to a boil, then reduce the heat, cover, and cook for 20 minutes on a simmer.
3. Fluff and mix the cooked quinoa with a fork and remove it from the heat.
4. Spread the quinoa in a baking stay.
5. Mix eggs, oats, onion, herbs, cheese, salt, and black pepper.
6. Stir in quinoa, then mix well. Make 4 patties out of this quinoa cheese mixture.
7. Divide the patties in the two crisper plates and spray them with cooking oil. 8. Return the crisper plates to the Ninja Foodi Dual Zone Air Fryer.
8. Choose the Air Fry mode for Zone 1 and set the temperature to 390 degrees F/ 200 degrees C and the time to 13 minutes.
9. Select the "MATCH" button to copy the settings for Zone 2.
10. Initiate cooking by pressing the START/STOP button.
11. Flip the patties once cooked halfway through, and resume cooking.
12. Meanwhile, prepare the cucumber yogurt dill sauce by mixing all of its ingredients in a mixing bowl.
13. Place each quinoa patty in a burger bun along with arugula leaves.
14. Serve with yogurt dill sauce.

Garlic Herbed Baked Potatoes

Servings: 4
Cooking Time: 45 Minutes
Ingredients:
- 4 large baking potatoes
- Salt and black pepper, to taste
- 2 teaspoons avocado oil
- Cheese
- 2 cups sour cream
- 1 teaspoon garlic clove, minced
- 1 teaspoon fresh dill
- 2 teaspoons chopped chives
- Salt and black pepper, to taste
- 2 teaspoons Worcestershire sauce

Directions:
1. Pierce the skin of the potatoes with a fork.
2. Season the potatoes with olive oil, salt, and black pepper.
3. Divide the potatoes into the air fryer baskets.
4. Now press 1 for zone 1 and set it to AIR FRY mode at 350 degrees F/ 175 degrees C, for 45 minutes.
5. Select the MATCH button for zone 2.
6. Meanwhile, take a bowl and mix all the cheese ingredients together.
7. Once the cooking cycle is complete, take out the potatoes and make a slit in-between each one.
8. Add the cheese mixture in the cavity and serve it hot.

Fried Artichoke Hearts

Servings: 6
Cooking Time: 10 Minutes
Ingredients:
- 3 cans Quartered Artichokes, drained
- ½ cup mayonnaise
- 1 cup panko breadcrumbs
- ⅓ cup grated Parmesan
- salt and black pepper to taste
- Parsley for garnish

Directions:
1. Mix mayonnaise with salt and black pepper and keep the sauce aside.
2. Spread panko breadcrumbs in a bowl.
3. Coat the artichoke pieces with the breadcrumbs.
4. As you coat the artichokes, place them in the two crisper plates in a single layer, then spray them with cooking oil.
5. Return the crisper plates to the Ninja Foodi Dual Zone Air Fryer.
6. Choose the Air Fry mode for Zone 1 and set the temperature to 375 degrees F/ 190 degrees C and the time to 10 minutes.
7. Select the "MATCH" button to copy the settings for Zone 2.
8. Initiate cooking by pressing the START/STOP button.
9. Flip the artichokes once cooked halfway through, then resume cooking.
10. Serve warm with mayo sauce.

Balsamic Vegetables

Servings: 4
Cooking Time: 13 Minutes
Ingredients:
- 125g asparagus, cut woody ends
- 88g mushrooms, halved
- 1 tbsp Dijon mustard
- 3 tbsp soy sauce
- 27g brown sugar
- 57ml balsamic vinegar
- 32g olive oil
- 1 zucchini, sliced
- 1 yellow squash, sliced
- 170g grape tomatoes
- Pepper
- Salt

Directions:
1. In a bowl, mix asparagus, tomatoes, oil, mustard, soy sauce, mushrooms, zucchini, squash, brown sugar, vinegar, pepper, and salt.
2. Cover the bowl and place it in the refrigerator for 45 minutes.
3. Insert a crisper plate in the Ninja Foodi air fryer baskets.
4. Add the vegetable mixture in both baskets.
5. Select zone 1, then select "air fry" mode and set the temperature to 390 degrees F for 12 minutes. Press "match" to match zone 2 settings to zone 1. Press "start/stop" to begin. Stir halfway through.

Nutrition:
- (Per serving) Calories 184 | Fat 13.3g |Sodium 778mg | Carbs 14.7g | Fiber 3.6g | Sugar 9.5g | Protein 5.5g

Bacon Potato Patties

Servings: 2
Cooking Time: 15 Minutes
Ingredients:
- 1 egg
- 600g mashed potatoes
- 119g breadcrumbs
- 2 bacon slices, cooked & chopped
- 235g cheddar cheese, shredded
- 15g flour
- Pepper
- Salt

Directions:
1. In a bowl, mix mashed potatoes with remaining ingredients until well combined.
2. Make patties from potato mixture and place on a plate.
3. Place plate in the refrigerator for 10 minutes
4. Insert a crisper plate in the Ninja Foodi air fryer baskets.
5. Place the prepared patties in both baskets.
6. Select zone 1 then select "air fry" mode and set the temperature to 390 degrees F for 15 minutes. Press "match" to match zone 2 settings to zone 1. Press "start/stop" to begin. Turn halfway through.

Nutrition:
- (Per serving) Calories 702 | Fat 26.8g |Sodium 1405mg | Carbs 84.8g | Fiber 2.7g | Sugar 3.8g | Protein 30.5g

Beets With Orange Gremolata And Goat's Cheese

Servings: 12
Cooking Time: 45 Minutes
Ingredients:
- 3 medium fresh golden beets (about 1 pound)
- 3 medium fresh beets (about 1 pound)
- 2 tablespoons lime juice
- 2 tablespoons orange juice
- ½ teaspoon fine sea salt
- 1 tablespoon minced fresh parsley
- 1 tablespoon minced fresh sage
- 1 garlic clove, minced
- 1 teaspoon grated orange zest
- 3 tablespoons crumbled goat's cheese
- 2 tablespoons sunflower kernels

Directions:
1. Scrub the beets and trim the tops by 1 inch.
2. Place the beets on a double thickness of heavy-duty foil . Fold the foil around the beets, sealing tightly.
3. Place a crisper plate in both drawers. Put the beets in a single layer in each drawer. Insert the drawers into the unit.
4. Select zone 1, then AIR FRY, then set the temperature to 360 degrees F/ 180 degrees C with a 45-minute timer. To match zone 2 settings to zone 1, choose MATCH. To begin, select START/STOP.
5. Remove the beets from the drawers after the timer has finished. Peel, halve, and slice them when they're cool enough to handle. Place them in a serving bowl.
6. Toss in the lime juice, orange juice, and salt to coat. Sprinkle the beets with the parsley, sage, garlic, and orange zest. The sunflower kernels and goat's cheese go on top.

Garlic Potato Wedges In Air Fryer

Servings: 2
Cooking Time: 23 Minutes
Ingredients:
- 4 medium potatoes, peeled and cut into wedges
- 4 tablespoons butter
- 1 teaspoon chopped cilantro
- 1 cup plain flour
- 1 teaspoon garlic, minced
- Salt and black pepper, to taste

Directions:
1. Soak the potato wedges in cold water for about 30 minutes.
2. Drain and pat dry with a paper towel.
3. Boil water in a large pot and boil the wedges for 3 minutes and place on a paper towel.
4. In a bowl, mix garlic, melted butter, salt, pepper, and cilantro.
5. Add the flour to a separate bowl along with the salt and black pepper.
6. Add water to the flour so it gets a runny in texture.
7. Coat the potatoes with the flour mixture and divide them into two foil tins. 8. Place the foil tins in each air fryer basket.
8. Set the zone 1 basket to AIR FRY mode at 390 degrees F/ 200 degrees C for 20 minutes.
9. Select the MATCH button for the zone 2 basket. 11. Once done, serve and enjoy.

Delicious Potatoes & Carrots

Servings: 8
Cooking Time: 25 Minutes
Ingredients:
- 453g carrots, sliced
- 2 tsp smoked paprika
- 21g sugar
- 30ml olive oil
- 453g potatoes, diced
- ¼ tsp thyme
- ½ tsp dried oregano
- 1 tsp garlic powder
- Pepper
- Salt

Directions:
1. In a bowl, toss carrots and potatoes with 1 tablespoon of oil.
2. Insert a crisper plate in the Ninja Foodi air fryer baskets.
3. Add carrots and potatoes to both baskets.
4. Select zone 1 then select "air fry" mode and set the temperature to 390 degrees F for 15 minutes. Press "match" to match zone 2 settings to zone 1. Press "start/stop" to begin.
5. In a mixing bowl, add cooked potatoes, carrots, smoked paprika, sugar, oil, thyme, oregano, garlic powder, pepper, and salt and toss well.
6. Return carrot and potato mixture into the air fryer basket and cook for 10 minutes more.

Nutrition:
- (Per serving) Calories 101 | Fat 3.6g |Sodium 62mg | Carbs 16.6g | Fiber 3g | Sugar 5.1g | Protein 1.6g

Jerk Tofu With Roasted Cabbage

Servings: 4
Cooking Time: 20 Minutes
Ingredients:
- FOR THE JERK TOFU
- 1 (14-ounce) package extra-firm tofu, drained
- 1 tablespoon apple cider vinegar
- 1 tablespoon reduced-sodium soy sauce
- 2 tablespoons jerk seasoning
- Juice of 1 lime
- ½ teaspoon kosher salt
- 2 tablespoons olive oil
- FOR THE CABBAGE
- 1 (14-ounce) bag coleslaw mix
- 1 red bell pepper, thinly sliced
- 2 scallions, thinly sliced
- 2 tablespoons water
- 3 garlic cloves, minced
- ¼ teaspoon fresh thyme leaves
- ¼ teaspoon onion powder
- ¼ teaspoon kosher salt
- ¼ teaspoon freshly ground black pepper

Directions:
1. To prep the jerk tofu: Cut the tofu horizontally into 4 slabs.
2. In a shallow dish (big enough to hold the tofu slabs), whisk together the vinegar, soy sauce, jerk seasoning, lime juice, and salt.
3. Place the tofu in the marinade and turn to coat both sides. Cover and marinate for at least 15 minutes (or up to overnight in the refrigerator).
4. To prep the cabbage: In the Zone 2 basket, combine the coleslaw, bell pepper, scallions, water, garlic, thyme, onion powder, salt, and black pepper.
5. To cook the tofu and cabbage: Install a crisper plate in the Zone 1 basket and add the tofu in a single layer. Brush the tofu with the oil and insert the basket in the unit. Insert the Zone 2 basket in the unit.
6. Select Zone 1, select AIR FRY, set the temperature to 390°F, and set the timer to 15 minutes.
7. Select Zone 2, select ROAST, set the temperature to 330°F, and set the timer to 20 minutes. Select SMART FINISH.
8. Press START/PAUSE to begin cooking.
9. When both timers read 5 minutes, press START/PAUSE. Remove the Zone 1 basket and use silicone-tipped tongs to flip the tofu. Reinsert the basket in the unit. Remove the Zone 2 basket and stir the cabbage. Reinsert the basket and press START/PAUSE to resume cooking.
10. When cooking is complete, the tofu will be crispy and browned around the edges and the cabbage soft.
11. Transfer the tofu to four plates and serve with the cabbage on the side.

Nutrition:
- (Per serving) Calories: 220; Total fat: 12g; Saturated fat: 1.5g; Carbohydrates: 21g; Fiber: 5g; Protein: 12g; Sodium: 817mg

Mushroom Roll-ups

Servings: 10
Cooking Time: 10 Minutes
Ingredients:
- 2 tablespoons extra virgin olive oil
- 8 ounces large portobello mushrooms (gills discarded), finely chopped
- 1 teaspoon dried oregano
- 1 teaspoon dried thyme
- ½ teaspoon crushed red pepper flakes
- ¼ teaspoon salt
- 8 ounces cream cheese, softened
- 4 ounces whole-milk ricotta cheese
- 10 flour tortillas (8-inch)
- Cooking spray
- Chutney, for serving (optional)

Directions:
1. Heat the oil in a pan over medium heat. Add the mushrooms and cook for 4 minutes. Sauté until the mushrooms are browned, about 4-6 minutes, with the oregano, thyme, pepper flakes, and salt. Cool.
2. Combine the cheeses in a mixing bowl| fold in the mushrooms until thoroughly combined.
3. On the bottom center of each tortilla, spread 3 tablespoons of the mushroom mixture. Tightly roll up each tortilla and secure with toothpicks.
4. Place a crisper plate in each drawer. Put the roll-ups in a single layer in each. Insert the drawers into the unit.
5. Select zone 1, then AIR FRY, then set the temperature to 400 degrees F/ 200 degrees C with a 10-minute timer. To match zone 2 settings to zone 1, choose MATCH. To begin, select START/STOP.
6. Remove the roll-ups from the drawers after the timer has finished. When they have cooled enough to handle, discard the toothpicks.
7. Serve and enjoy!

Chickpea Fritters

Servings: 6
Cooking Time: 6 Minutes
Ingredients:
- 237ml plain yogurt
- 2 tablespoons sugar
- 1 tablespoon honey
- ½ teaspoon salt
- ½ teaspoon black pepper
- ½ teaspoon crushed red pepper flakes
- 1 can (28g) chickpeas, drained
- 1 teaspoon ground cumin
- ½ teaspoon salt
- ½ teaspoon garlic powder
- ½ teaspoon ground ginger
- 1 large egg
- ½ teaspoon baking soda
- ½ cup fresh coriander, chopped
- 2 green onions, sliced

Directions:
1. Mash chickpeas with rest of the ingredients in a food processor.
2. Layer the two air fryer baskets with a parchment paper.
3. Drop the batter in the baskets spoon by spoon.
4. Return the air fryer basket 1 to Zone 1, and basket 2 to Zone 2 of the Ninja Foodi 2-Basket Air Fryer.
5. Choose the "Air Fry" mode for Zone 1 at 400 degrees F and 6 minutes of cooking time.
6. Select the "MATCH COOK" option to copy the settings for Zone 2.
7. Initiate cooking by pressing the START/PAUSE BUTTON.
8. Flip the fritters once cooked halfway through.
9. Serve warm.

Nutrition:
- (Per serving) Calories 284 | Fat 7.9g | Sodium 704mg | Carbs 38.1g | Fiber 1.9g | Sugar 1.9g | Protein 14.8g

Beef, Pork, And Lamb Recipes

Pork Chops With Brussels Sprouts

Servings: 4
Cooking Time: 15 Minutes.
Ingredients:
- 4 bone-in center-cut pork chop
- Cooking spray
- Salt, to taste
- Black pepper, to taste
- 2 teaspoons olive oil
- 2 teaspoons pure maple syrup
- 2 teaspoons Dijon mustard
- 6 ounces Brussels sprouts, quartered

Directions:
1. Rub pork chop with salt, ¼ teaspoons black pepper, and cooking spray.
2. Toss Brussels sprouts with mustard, syrup, oil, ¼ teaspoon of black pepper in a medium bowl.
3. Add pork chop to the crisper plate of Zone 1 of the Ninja Foodi Dual Zone Air Fryer.
4. Return the crisper plate to the Ninja Foodi Dual Zone Air Fryer.
5. Choose the Air Fry mode for Zone 1 and set the temperature to 400 degrees F and the time to 15 minutes.
6. Add the Brussels sprouts to the crisper plate of Zone 2 and return it to the unit.
7. Choose the Air Fry mode for Zone 2 with 350 degrees F and the time to 13 minutes.
8. Press the SYNC button to sync the finish time for both Zones.
9. Initiate cooking by pressing the START/STOP button.
10. Serve warm and fresh

Nutrition:
- (Per serving) Calories 336 | Fat 27.1g | Sodium 66mg | Carbs 1.1g | Fiber 0.4g | Sugar 0.2g | Protein 19.7g

Sausage-stuffed Peppers

Servings: 6
Cooking Time: 28 To 30 Minutes
Ingredients:
- Avocado oil spray
- 230 g Italian-seasoned sausage, casings removed
- 120 ml chopped mushrooms
- 60 ml diced onion
- 1 teaspoon Italian seasoning
- Sea salt and freshly ground black pepper, to taste
- 235 ml keto-friendly marinara sauce
- 3 peppers, halved and seeded
- 85 g low-moisture Mozzarella or other melting cheese, shredded

Directions:
1. Spray a large skillet with oil and place it over medium-high heat. Add the sausage and cook for 5 minutes, breaking up the meat with a wooden spoon. Add the mushrooms, onion, and Italian seasoning, and season with salt and pepper. Cook for 5 minutes more. Stir in the marinara sauce and cook until heated through.
2. Scoop the sausage filling into the pepper halves.
3. Set the air fryer to 176°C. Arrange the peppers in a single layer in the two air fryer drawers. Air fry for 15 minutes.
4. Top the stuffed peppers with the cheese and air fry for 3 to 5 minutes more, until the cheese is melted and the peppers are tender.

New York Strip Steak

Servings: 2
Cooking Time: 10 Minutes
Ingredients:
- 1 (4½-ounce) New York strip steaks
- 1½ teaspoons olive oil
- Salt and ground black pepper, as required

Directions:
1. Grease each basket of "Zone 1" and "Zone 2" of Ninja Foodi 2-Basket Air Fryer.
2. Press "Zone 1" and "Zone 2" and then rotate the knob for each zone to select "Air Fry".
3. Set the temperature to 400 degrees F/ 200 degrees C for both zones and then set the time for 5 minutes to preheat.
4. Coat the steaks with oil and then sprinkle with salt and black pepper evenly.
5. After preheating, arrange the steak into the basket of each zone.
6. Slide each basket into Air Fryer and set the time for 10 minutes.
7. While cooking, flip the steak once halfway through.
8. After cooking time is completed, remove the steaks from Air Fryer and place onto a platter for about 10 minutes.
9. Cut each steak into desired size slices and serve immediately.

Glazed Steak Recipe

Servings:2
Cooking Time:25
Ingredients:
- 1 pound of beef steaks
- ½ cup, soy sauce
- Salt and black pepper, to taste
- 1 tablespoon of vegetable oil
- 1 teaspoon of grated ginger
- 4 cloves garlic, minced
- 1/4 cup brown sugar

Directions:
1. Take a bowl and whisk together soy sauce, salt, pepper, vegetable oil, garlic, brown sugar, and ginger.
2. Once a paste is made rub the steak with the marinate
3. Let it sit for 30 minutes.
4. After 30 minutes add the steak to the air fryer basket and set it to AIR BROIL mode at 400 degrees F for 18-22 minutes.
5. After 10 minutes, hit pause and takeout the basket.
6. Let the steak flip and again let it AIR BROIL for the remaining minutes.
7. Once 25 minutes of cooking cycle completes.
8. Take out the steak and let it rest. Serve by cutting into slices.
9. Enjoy.

Nutrition:
- (Per serving) Calories 563| Fat 21 g| Sodium 156mg | Carbs 20.6g | Fiber0.3 g| Sugar17.8 g | Protein69.4 g

Sausage And Cauliflower Arancini

Servings: 6
Cooking Time: 28 To 32 Minutes
Ingredients:
- Avocado oil spray
- 170 g Italian-seasoned sausage, casings removed
- 60 ml diced onion
- 1 teaspoon minced garlic
- 1 teaspoon dried thyme
- Sea salt and freshly ground black pepper, to taste
- 120 ml cauliflower rice
- 85 g cream cheese
- 110 g Cheddar cheese, shredded
- 1 large egg
- 120 ml finely ground blanched almond flour
- 60 ml finely grated Parmesan cheese
- Keto-friendly marinara sauce, for serving

Directions:
1. Spray a large skillet with oil and place it over medium-high heat. Once the skillet is hot, put the sausage in the skillet and cook for 7 minutes, breaking up the meat with the back of a spoon.
2. Reduce the heat to medium and add the onion. Cook for 5 minutes, then add the garlic, thyme, and salt and pepper to taste. Cook for 1 minute more.
3. Add the cauliflower rice and cream cheese to the skillet. Cook for 7 minutes, stirring frequently, until the cream cheese melts and the cauliflower is tender.
4. Remove the skillet from the heat and stir in the Cheddar cheese. Using a cookie scoop, form the mixture into 1½-inch balls. Place the balls on a parchment paper-lined baking sheet. Freeze for 30 minutes.
5. Place the egg in a shallow bowl and beat it with a fork. In a separate bowl, stir together the almond flour and Parmesan cheese.
6. Dip the cauliflower balls into the egg, then coat them with the almond flour mixture, gently pressing the mixture to the balls to adhere.
7. Set the air fryer to 204°C. Spray the cauliflower rice balls with oil, and arrange them in a single layer in the two air fryer drawers. Air fry for 5 minutes. Flip the rice balls and spray them with more oil. Air fry for 3 to 7 minutes longer, until the balls are golden brown.
8. Serve warm with marinara sauce.

Bacon-wrapped Vegetable Kebabs

Servings: 4
Cooking Time: 10 To 12 Minutes
Ingredients:
- 110 g mushrooms, sliced
- 1 small courgette, sliced
- 12 baby plum tomatoes
- 110 g sliced bacon, halved
- Avocado oil spray
- Sea salt and freshly ground black pepper, to taste

Directions:
1. Stack 3 mushroom slices, 1 courgette slice, and 1 tomato. Wrap a bacon strip around the vegetables and thread them onto a skewer. Repeat with the remaining vegetables and bacon. Spray with oil and sprinkle with salt and pepper.
2. Set the air fryer to 204°C. Place the skewers in the two air fryer drawers in a single layer and air fry for 5 minutes. Flip the skewers and cook for 5 to 7 minutes more, until the bacon is crispy and the vegetables are tender.
3. Serve warm.

Sausage Meatballs

Servings: 24
Cooking Time: 30 Minutes
Ingredients:
- 1 egg, lightly beaten
- 900g pork sausage
- 29g breadcrumbs
- 100g pimientos, drained & diced
- 1 tsp curry powder
- 1 tbsp garlic, minced
- 30ml olive oil
- 1 tbsp fresh rosemary, minced
- 25g parsley, minced
- Pepper
- Salt

Directions:
1. In a bowl, add pork sausage and remaining ingredients and mix until well combined.
2. Insert a crisper plate in the Ninja Foodi air fryer baskets.
3. Make small balls from the meat mixture and place them in both baskets.
4. Select zone 1 then select "air fry" mode and set the temperature to 390 degrees F for 10 minutes. Press "match" to match zone 2 settings to zone 1. Press "start/stop" to begin.

Stuffed Beef Fillet With Feta Cheese

Servings: 4
Cooking Time: 10 Minutes
Ingredients:
- 680 g beef fillet, pounded to ¼ inch thick
- 3 teaspoons sea salt
- 1 teaspoon ground black pepper
- 60 g creamy goat cheese
- 120 ml crumbled feta cheese
- 60 ml finely chopped onions
- 2 cloves garlic, minced
- Cooking spray

Directions:
1. Preheat the air fryer to 204°C. Spritz the two air fryer drawers with cooking spray. 2. Unfold the beef on a clean work surface. Rub the salt and pepper all over the beef to season. 3. Make the filling for the stuffed beef fillet: Combine the goat cheese, feta, onions, and garlic in a medium bowl. Stir until well blended. 4. Spoon the mixture in the center of the fillet. Roll the fillet up tightly like rolling a burrito and use some kitchen twine to tie the fillet. 5. Arrange the fillet in the two air fryer drawers and air fry for 10 minutes, flipping the fillet halfway through to ensure even cooking, or until an instant-read thermometer inserted in the center of the fillet registers 57°C for medium-rare. 6. Transfer to a platter and serve immediately.

Filet Mignon Wrapped In Bacon

Servings: 2
Cooking Time: 20 Minutes
Ingredients:
- 2 (2-ounce) filet mignon
- 2 bacon slices
- Olive oil cooking spray
- Salt and ground black pepper, as required

Directions:
1. Wrap 1 bacon slice around each filet mignon and secure with toothpicks.
2. Season the filets with salt and black pepper lightly.
3. Grease each basket of "Zone 1" and "Zone 2" of Ninja Foodi 2-Basket Air Fryer.
4. Press "Zone 1" and "Zone 2" and then rotate the knob for each zone to select "Air Fry".
5. Set the temperature to 400 degrees F/ 200 degrees C for both zones and then set the time for 5 minutes to preheat.
6. After preheating, arrange the filets into the basket of each zone.
7. Slide each basket into Air Fryer and set the time for 15 minutes.
8. While cooking, flip the filets once halfway through.
9. After cooking time is completed, remove the filets from Air Fryer and serve hot.

Steak Fajitas With Onions And Peppers

Servings: 6
Cooking Time: 15 Minutes
Ingredients:
- 1 pound steak
- 1 green bell pepper, sliced
- 1 yellow bell pepper, sliced
- 1 red bell pepper, sliced
- ½ cup sliced white onions
- 1 packet gluten-free fajita seasoning
- Olive oil spray

Directions:
1. Thinly slice the steak against the grain. These should be about ¼-inch slices.
2. Mix the steak with the peppers and onions.
3. Evenly coat with the fajita seasoning.
4. Install a crisper plate in both drawers. Place half the steak mixture in the zone 1 drawer and half in zone 2's, then insert the drawers into the unit.
5. Select zone 1, select AIR FRY, set temperature to 390 degrees F/ 200 degrees C, and set time to 15 minutes. Select MATCH to match zone 2 settings to zone 1. Press the START/STOP button to begin cooking.
6. When the time reaches 10 minutes, press START/STOP to pause the unit. Remove the drawers and flip the steak strips. Re-insert the drawers into the unit and press START/STOP to resume cooking.
7. Serve in warm tortillas.

Nutrition:
- (Per serving) Calories 305 | Fat 17g | Sodium 418mg | Carbs 15g | Fiber 2g | Sugar 4g | Protein 22g

Beef Cheeseburgers

Servings: 4
Cooking Time: 13 Minutes.
Ingredients:
- 1 lb. ground beef
- Salt, to taste
- 2 garlic cloves, minced
- 1 tablespoon soy sauce
- Black pepper, to taste
- 4 American cheese slices
- 4 hamburger buns
- Mayonnaise, to serve
- Lettuce, to serve
- Sliced tomatoes, to serve
- Sliced red onion, to serve

Directions:
1. Mix beef with soy sauce and garlic in a large bowl.
2. Make 4 patties of 4 inches in diameter.
3. Rub them with salt and black pepper on both sides.
4. Place the 2 patties in each of the crisper plate.
5. Return the crisper plate to the Ninja Foodi Dual Zone Air Fryer.
6. Choose the Air Fry mode for Zone 1 and set the temperature to 390 degrees F and the time to 13 minutes.
7. Select the "MATCH" button to copy the settings for Zone 2.
8. Initiate cooking by pressing the START/STOP button.
9. Flip each patty once cooked halfway through, and resume cooking.
10. Add each patty to the hamburger buns along with mayo, tomatoes, onions, and lettuce.
11. Serve.

Nutrition:
- (Per serving) Calories 437 | Fat 28g |Sodium 1221mg | Carbs 22.3g | Fiber 0.9g | Sugar 8g | Protein 30.3g

Kielbasa Sausage With Pineapple And Kheema Meatloaf

Servings: 6 To 8
Cooking Time: 15 Minutes
Ingredients:
- Kielbasa Sausage with Pineapple:
- 340 g kielbasa sausage, cut into ½-inch slices
- 1 (230 g) can pineapple chunks in juice, drained
- 235 ml pepper chunks
- 1 tablespoon barbecue seasoning
- 1 tablespoon soy sauce
- Cooking spray
- Kheema Meatloaf:
- 450 g 85% lean beef mince
- 2 large eggs, lightly beaten
- 235 ml diced brown onion
- 60 ml chopped fresh coriander
- 1 tablespoon minced fresh ginger
- 1 tablespoon minced garlic
- 2 teaspoons garam masala
- 1 teaspoon coarse or flaky salt
- 1 teaspoon ground turmeric
- 1 teaspoon cayenne pepper
- ½ teaspoon ground cinnamon
- ⅛ teaspoon ground cardamom

Directions:
1. Make the Kielbasa Sausage with Pineapple :
2. Preheat the air fryer to 200ºC. Spritz the zone 1 air fryer drawer with cooking spray.
3. Combine all the ingredients in a large bowl. Toss to mix well.
4. Pour the sausage mixture in the preheated zone 1 air fryer drawer.
5. Air fry for 10 minutes or until the sausage is lightly browned and the pepper and pineapple are soft. Shake the drawer halfway through. Serve immediately.
6. Make the Kheema Meatloaf :
7. In a large bowl, gently mix the beef mince, eggs, onion, coriander, ginger, garlic, garam masala, salt, turmeric, cayenne, cinnamon, and cardamom until thoroughly combined.
8. Place the seasoned meat in a baking pan. Place the pan in the zone 2 air fryer drawer. Set the temperature to 176ºC for 15 minutes. Use a meat thermometer to ensure the meat loaf has reached an internal temperature of 72ºC .
9. Drain the fat and liquid from the pan and let stand for 5 minutes before slicing.
10. Slice and serve hot.

Seasoned Flank Steak

Servings: 12
Cooking Time: 30 Minutes
Ingredients:
- 2 (2-pound) flank steaks
- 3 tablespoons taco seasoning rub

Directions:
1. Grease each basket of "Zone 1" and "Zone 2" of Ninja Foodi 2-Basket Air Fryer.
2. Press "Zone 1" and "Zone 2" and then rotate the knob for each zone to select "Bake".
3. Set the temperature to 420 degrees F/ 215 degrees C for both zones and then set the time for 5 minutes to preheat.
4. Rub the steaks with taco seasoning evenly.
5. After preheating, arrange 1 steak into the basket of each zone.
6. Slide each basket into Air Fryer and set the time for 30 minutes.
7. After cooking time is completed, remove the steaks from Air Fryer and place onto a cutting board for about 10-15 minutes before slicing.
8. With a sharp knife, cut each steak into desired size slices and serve.

Simple Strip Steak

Servings: 4
Cooking Time: 10 Minutes
Ingredients:
- 2 (9½-ounce) New York strip steaks
- Salt and ground black pepper, as required
- 3 teaspoons olive oil

Directions:
1. Grease each basket of "Zone 1" and "Zone 2" of Ninja Foodi 2-Basket Air Fryer.
2. Press "Zone 1" and "Zone 2" and then rotate the knob for each zone to select "Air Fry".
3. Set the temperature to 400 degrees F/ 200 degrees C for both zones and then set the time for 5 minutes to preheat.
4. Coat the steaks with oil and then sprinkle with salt and black pepper evenly.
5. After preheating, arrange 1 steak into the basket of each zone.
6. Slide each basket into Air Fryer and set the time for 10 minutes.
7. While cooking, flip the steak once halfway through.
8. After cooking time is completed, remove the steaks from Air Fryer and place onto a platter for about 10 minutes.
9. Cut each steak into desired size slices and serve immediately.

Pork Chops With Broccoli

Servings: 2
Cooking Time: 13 Minutes.
Ingredients:
- 2 (5 ounces) bone-in pork chops
- 2 tablespoons avocado oil
- ½ teaspoon paprika
- ½ teaspoon onion powder
- ½ teaspoon garlic powder
- 1 teaspoon salt
- 2 cups broccoli florets
- 2 garlic cloves, minced

Directions:
1. Rub the pork chops with avocado oil, garlic, paprika, and spices.
2. Add pork chop to the crisper plate of Zone 1 in the Ninja Foodi Dual Zone Air Fryer.
3. Return the crisper plate to the Air Fryer.
4. Choose the Air Fry mode for Zone 1 and set the temperature to 400 degrees F and the time to 12 minutes.
5. Add the broccoli to the Zone 2 drawer and return it to the unit.
6. Choose the Air Fry mode for Zone 2 with 375 degrees F and the time to 13 minutes.
7. Press the SYNC button to sync the finish time for both Zones.
8. Initiate cooking by pressing the START/STOP button.
9. Flip the pork once cooked halfway through.
10. Cut the hardened butter into the cubes and place them on top of the pork chops.
11. Serve warm with crispy broccoli florets

Nutrition:
- (Per serving) Calories 410 | Fat 17.8g |Sodium 619mg | Carbs 21g | Fiber 1.4g | Sugar 1.8g | Protein 38.4g

Steak Bites With Cowboy Butter

Servings: 4
Cooking Time: 20 Minutes
Ingredients:
- 455g steak sirloin
- Cooking spray
- Cowboy butter sauce
- 1 stick salted butter melted
- 1 tablespoon lemon zest
- 1 tablespoon lemon juice
- ½ teaspoon garlic powder
- ¼ teaspoon red pepper flakes
- ½ teaspoon sea salt
- ½ teaspoon black pepper
- ½ tablespoon Dijon mustard
- ½ teaspoon Worcestershire sauce
- 1 tablespoon parsley freshly chopped

Directions:
1. Mix all the cowboy butter ingredients in a bowl.
2. Stir in steak cubes and mix well.
3. Cover and marinate in the refrigerator for 1 hour.
4. Divide the steak cubes in the air fryer baskets then use cooking spray.
5. Return the air fryer basket 1 to Zone 1, and basket 2 to Zone 2 of the Ninja Foodi 2-Basket Air Fryer.
6. Choose the "Air Fry" mode for Zone 1 at 400 degrees F and 15 minutes of cooking time.
7. Select the "MATCH COOK" option to copy the settings for Zone 2.
8. Initiate cooking by pressing the START/PAUSE BUTTON.
9. Serve warm.

Mojito Lamb Chops

Servings: 2
Cooking Time: 5 Minutes
Ingredients:
- Marinade:
- 2 teaspoons grated lime zest
- 120 ml lime juice
- 60 ml avocado oil
- 60 ml chopped fresh mint leaves
- 4 cloves garlic, roughly chopped
- 2 teaspoons fine sea salt
- ½ teaspoon ground black pepper
- 4 (1-inch-thick) lamb chops
- Sprigs of fresh mint, for garnish (optional)
- Lime slices, for serving (optional)

Directions:
1. Make the marinade: Place all the ingredients for the marinade in a food processor or blender and purée until mostly smooth with a few small chunks. Transfer half of the marinade to a shallow dish and set the other half aside for serving. Add the lamb to the shallow dish, cover, and place in the refrigerator to marinate for at least 2 hours or overnight. 2. Spray the two air fryer drawers with avocado oil. Preheat the air fryer to 200ºC. 3. Remove the chops from the marinade and place them in the two air fryer drawers. Air fry for 5 minutes, or until the internal temperature reaches 64ºC for medium doneness. 4. Allow the chops to rest for 10 minutes before serving with the rest of the marinade as a sauce. Garnish with fresh mint leaves and serve with lime slices, if desired. Best served fresh.

Sumptuous Pizza Tortilla Rolls

Servings: 4
Cooking Time: 6 Minutes
Ingredients:
- 1 teaspoon butter
- ½ medium onion, slivered
- ½ red or green pepper, julienned
- 110 g fresh white mushrooms, chopped
- 120 ml pizza sauce
- 8 flour tortillas
- 8 thin slices wafer-thin ham
- 24 pepperoni slices
- 235 ml shredded Mozzarella cheese
- Cooking spray

Directions:
1. Preheat the air fryer to 200ºC.
2. Put butter, onions, pepper, and mushrooms in a baking pan. Bake in the preheated air fryer for 3 minutes. Stir and cook 3 to 4 minutes longer until just crisp and tender. Remove pan and set aside.
3. To assemble rolls, spread about 2 teaspoons of pizza sauce on one half of each tortilla. Top with a slice of ham and 3 slices of pepperoni. Divide sautéed vegetables among tortillas and top with cheese.
4. Roll up tortillas, secure with toothpicks if needed, and spray with oil.
5. Put the rolls in the two air fryer drawers and air fry for 4 minutes. Turn and air fry 4 minutes, until heated through and lightly browned.
6. Serve immediately.

Tomahawk Steak

Servings: 4
Cooking Time: 12 Minutes
Ingredients:
- 4 tablespoons butter, softened
- 2 cloves garlic, minced
- 2 teaspoons chopped fresh parsley
- 1 teaspoon chopped chives
- 1 teaspoon chopped fresh thyme
- 1 teaspoon chopped fresh rosemary
- 2 (2 pounds each) bone-in ribeye steaks
- Kosher salt, to taste
- Freshly ground black pepper, to taste

Directions:
1. In a small bowl, combine the butter and herbs. Place the mixture in the center of a piece of plastic wrap and roll it into a log. Twist the ends together to keep it tight and refrigerate until hardened, about 20 minutes.
2. Season the steaks on both sides with salt and pepper.
3. Install a crisper plate in both drawers. Place one steak in the zone 1 drawer and one in zone 2's, then insert the drawers into the unit.
4. Select zone 1, select AIR FRY, set temperature to 390 degrees F/ 200 degrees C, and set time to 12 minutes. Select MATCH to match zone 2 settings to zone 1. Press the START/STOP button to begin cooking.
5. When the time reaches 10 minutes, press START/STOP to pause the unit. Remove the drawers and flip the steaks. Add the herb-butter to the tops of the steaks. Re-insert the drawers into the unit and press START/STOP to resume cooking.
6. Serve and enjoy!

Nutrition:
- (Per serving) Calories 338 | Fat 21.2g | Sodium 1503mg | Carbs 5.1g | Fiber 0.3g | Sugar 4.6g | Protein 29.3g

Roast Souvlaki-style Pork With Lemon-feta Baby Potatoes

Servings:4
Cooking Time: 40 Minutes
Ingredients:
- FOR THE PORK
- 1½ pounds pork tenderloin, cut into bite-size cubes
- ¼ cup olive oil
- ¼ cup fresh lemon juice
- 2 teaspoons minced garlic
- 2 teaspoons honey
- 1½ teaspoons dried oregano
- ¼ teaspoon kosher salt
- ¼ teaspoon freshly ground black pepper
- FOR THE POTATOES
- 1 pound baby red or yellow potatoes, halved
- 1 tablespoon olive oil
- Grated zest and juice of 1 lemon
- ½ teaspoon kosher salt
- ¼ teaspoon freshly ground black pepper
- ⅓ cup crumbled feta cheese
- 2 tablespoons chopped fresh parsley

Directions:
1. To prep the pork: In a large bowl, combine the pork, oil, lemon juice, garlic, honey, oregano, salt, and black pepper. If desired, cover and refrigerate up to 24 hours.
2. To prep the potatoes: In a large bowl, combine the potatoes, oil, lemon zest, lemon juice, salt, and black pepper. Mix to coat the potatoes.
3. To cook the pork and potatoes: Install a crisper plate in each of the two baskets. Place the pork in the Zone 1 basket and insert the basket in the unit. Place the potatoes in the Zone 2 basket and insert the basket in the unit.
4. Select Zone 1, select ROAST, set the temperature to 390°F, and set the time to 20 minutes.
5. Select Zone 2, select AIR FRY, set the temperature to 400°F, and set the time to 40 minutes. Select SMART FINISH.
6. Press START/PAUSE to begin cooking.
7. When cooking is complete, the pork will be cooked through (an instant-read thermometer should read 145°F) and the potatoes will be tender and beginning to brown around the edges.
8. Stir the feta and parsley into the potatoes. Serve the pork and potatoes while hot.

Nutrition:
- (Per serving) Calories: 395; Total fat: 17g; Saturated fat: 4.5g; Carbohydrates: 24g; Fiber: 2g; Protein: 37g; Sodium: 399mg

Lamb Shank With Mushroom Sauce

Servings: 4
Cooking Time: 35 Minutes.

Ingredients:
- 20 mushrooms, chopped
- 2 red bell pepper, chopped
- 2 red onion, chopped
- 1 cup red wine
- 4 leeks, chopped
- 6 tablespoons balsamic vinegar
- 2 teaspoons black pepper
- 2 teaspoons salt
- 3 tablespoons fresh rosemary
- 6 garlic cloves
- 4 lamb shanks
- 3 tablespoons olive oil

Directions:
1. Season the lamb shanks with salt, pepper, rosemary, and 1 teaspoon of olive oil.
2. Set half of the shanks in each of the crisper plate.
3. Return the crisper plate to the Ninja Foodi Dual Zone Air Fryer.
4. Choose the Air Fry mode for Zone 1 and set the temperature to 390 degrees F and the time to 25 minutes.
5. Select the "MATCH" button to copy the settings for Zone 2.
6. Initiate cooking by pressing the START/STOP button.
7. Flip the shanks halfway through, and resume cooking.
8. Meanwhile, add and heat the remaining olive oil in a skillet.
9. Add onion and garlic to sauté for 5 minutes.
10. Add in mushrooms and cook for 5 minutes.
11. Add red wine and cook until it is absorbed
12. Stir all the remaining vegetables along with black pepper and salt.
13. Cook until vegetables are al dente.
14. Serve the air fried shanks with sautéed vegetable fry.

Nutrition:
- (Per serving) Calories 352 | Fat 9.1g |Sodium 1294mg | Carbs 3.9g | Fiber 1g | Sugar 1g | Protein 61g

Korean Bbq Beef

Servings: 6
Cooking Time: 30 Minutes

Ingredients:
- For the meat:
- 1 pound flank steak or thinly sliced steak
- ¼ cup corn starch
- Coconut oil spray
- For the sauce:
- ½ cup soy sauce or gluten-free soy sauce
- ½ cup brown sugar
- 2 tablespoons white wine vinegar
- 1 clove garlic, crushed
- 1 tablespoon hot chili sauce
- 1 teaspoon ground ginger
- ½ teaspoon sesame seeds
- 1 tablespoon corn starch
- 1 tablespoon water

Directions:
1. To begin, prepare the steak. Thinly slice it in that toss it in the corn starch to be coated thoroughly. Spray the tops with some coconut oil.
2. Spray the crisping plates and drawers with the coconut oil.
3. Place the crisping plates into the drawers. Place the steak strips into each drawer. Insert both drawers into the unit.
4. Select zone 1, Select AIR FRY, set the temperature to 375 degrees F/ 190 degrees C, and set time to 30 minutes. Select MATCH to match zone 2 settings with zone 1. Press the START/STOP button to begin cooking.
5. While the steak is cooking, add the sauce ingredients EXCEPT for the corn starch and water to a medium saucepan.
6. Warm it up to a low boil, then whisk in the corn starch and water.
7. Carefully remove the steak and pour the sauce over. Mix well.

Nutrition:
- (Per serving) Calories 500 | Fat 19.8g | Sodium 680mg | Carbs 50.1g | Fiber 4.1g | Sugar 0g | Protein 27.9g

Pigs In A Blanket With Spinach-artichoke Stuffed Mushrooms

Servings: 4
Cooking Time: 15 Minutes

Ingredients:
- FOR THE PIGS IN A BLANKET
- Half an 8-ounce tube refrigerated crescent roll dough
- 4 hot dogs
- ½ teaspoon everything bagel seasoning (optional)
- FOR THE STUFFED MUSHROOMS
- 1 cup frozen chopped spinach, thawed and drained
- 1 (14-ounce) can artichoke hearts, drained and chopped
- 2 ounces (¼ cup) cream cheese, at room temperature
- ¼ cup grated Parmesan cheese
- ½ teaspoon garlic powder
- 1 (8-ounce) package whole cremini mushrooms, stems removed

Directions:
1. To prep the pigs in a blanket: Unroll the crescent roll dough. It will be scored into 4 triangular pieces, but leave them in place and pinch together at the seams to form 1 large square of dough. Cut the dough into 4 strips.
2. Wrap one strip of dough around each hot dog, starting with a short end of the strips and wrapping in a spiral motion around the hot dog. If desired, sprinkle each pig in a blanket with everything bagel seasoning.
3. To prep the stuffed mushrooms: In a medium bowl, combine the spinach, artichoke hearts, cream cheese, Parmesan, and garlic powder. Stuff about 1 tablespoon of filling into each mushroom cap.
4. To cook the pigs in a blanket and mushrooms: Install a crisper plate in each of the two baskets. Place the pigs in a blanket in the Zone 1 basket and insert the basket in the unit. Place the mushrooms in the Zone 2 basket and insert the basket in the unit.
5. Select Zone 1, select AIR FRY, set the temperature to 370°F, and set the time to 8 minutes.
6. Select Zone 2, select BAKE, set the temperature to 370°F, and set the time to 15 minutes. Select SMART FINISH.
7. Press START/PAUSE to begin cooking.
8. When cooking is complete, the crescent roll dough should be cooked through and golden brown, and the mushrooms should be tender.

Nutrition:
- (Per serving) Calories: 371; Total fat: 25g; Saturated fat: 11g; Carbohydrates: 22g; Fiber: 2.5g; Protein: 14g; Sodium: 1,059mg

Steak And Asparagus Bundles

Servings: 6
Cooking Time: 10 Minutes

Ingredients:
- 907g flank steak, cut into 6 pieces
- Salt and black pepper, to taste
- ½ cup tamari sauce
- 2 cloves garlic, crushed
- 455g asparagus, trimmed
- 3 capsicums, sliced
- ¼ cup balsamic vinegar
- 79 ml beef broth
- 2 tablespoons unsalted butter
- Olive oil spray

Directions:
1. Mix steaks with black pepper, tamari sauce, and garlic in a Ziplock bag.
2. Seal the bag, shake well and refrigerate for 1 hour.
3. Place the steaks on the working surface and top each with asparagus and capsicums.
4. Roll the steaks and secure them with toothpicks.
5. Place these rolls in the air fryer baskets.
6. Return the air fryer basket 1 to Zone 1, and basket 2 to Zone 2 of the Ninja Foodi 2-Basket Air Fryer.
7. Choose the "Air Fry" mode for Zone 1 and set the temperature to 400 degrees F and 10 minutes of cooking time.
8. Select the "MATCH COOK" option to copy the settings for Zone 2.
9. Initiate cooking by pressing the START/PAUSE BUTTON.
10. Meanwhile, cook broth with butter and vinegar in a saucepan.
11. Cook this mixture until reduced by half and adjust seasoning with black pepper and salt.
12. Serve the steak rolls with the prepared sauce.

Tasty Lamb Patties

Servings: 8
Cooking Time: 12 Minutes
Ingredients:
- 900g ground lamb
- 1 tbsp ground coriander
- 4g fresh parsley, chopped
- 1 tsp garlic, minced
- ½ tsp cinnamon
- 1 tsp paprika
- 1 tbsp ground cumin
- Pepper
- Salt

Directions:
1. Add ground meat and remaining ingredients into a bowl and mix until well combined.
2. Insert a crisper plate in the Ninja Foodi air fryer baskets.
3. Make patties from the meat mixture and place in both baskets.
4. Select zone 1, then select "air fry" mode and set the temperature to 390 degrees F for 12 minutes. Press "match" to match zone 2 settings to zone 1. Press "start/stop" to begin. Turn halfway through.

Mozzarella Stuffed Beef And Pork Meatballs

Servings: 4 To 6
Cooking Time: 12 Minutes
Ingredients:
- 1 tablespoon olive oil
- 1 small onion, finely chopped
- 1 to 2 cloves garlic, minced
- 340 g beef mince
- 340 g pork mince
- 180 ml bread crumbs
- 60 ml grated Parmesan cheese
- 60 ml finely chopped fresh parsley
- ½ teaspoon dried oregano
- 1½ teaspoons salt
- Freshly ground black pepper, to taste
- 2 eggs, lightly beaten
- 140 g low-moisture Mozzarella or other melting cheese, cut into 1-inch cubes

Directions:
1. Preheat a skillet over medium-high heat. Add the oil and cook the onion and garlic until tender, but not browned. 2. Transfer the onion and garlic to a large bowl and add the beef, pork, bread crumbs, Parmesan cheese, parsley, oregano, salt, pepper and eggs. Mix well until all the ingredients are combined. Divide the mixture into 12 evenly sized balls. Make one meatball at a time, by pressing a hole in the meatball mixture with the finger and pushing a piece of Mozzarella cheese into the hole. Mold the meat back into a ball, enclosing the cheese. 3. Preheat the air fryer to 192°C. 4. Transfer meatballs to the two air fryer drawers and air fry for 12 minutes, shaking the drawers and turning the meatballs twice during the cooking process. Serve warm.

Air Fryer Chicken-fried Steak

Servings: 4
Cooking Time: 20 Minutes
Ingredients:
- 450 g beef braising steak
- 700 ml low-fat milk, divided
- 1 teaspoon dried thyme
- 1 teaspoon dried rosemary
- 2 medium egg whites
- 235 ml gluten-free breadcrumbs
- 120 ml coconut flour
- 1 tablespoon Cajun seasoning

Directions:
1. In a bowl, marinate the steak in 475 ml of milk for 30 to 45 minutes.
2. Remove the steak from milk, shake off the excess liquid, and season with the thyme and rosemary. Discard the milk.
3. In a shallow bowl, beat the egg whites with the remaining 235 ml of milk.
4. In a separate shallow bowl, combine the breadcrumbs, coconut flour, and seasoning.
5. Dip the steak in the egg white mixture then dredge in the breadcrumb mixture, coating well.
6. Place the steak in the zone 1 drawer of an air fryer.
7. Set the temperature to 200°C, close, and cook for 10 minutes.
8. Open the air fryer, turn the steaks, close, and cook for 10 minutes. Let rest for 5 minutes.

Garlic-rosemary Pork Loin With Scalloped Potatoes And Cauliflower

Servings: 6
Cooking Time: 50 Minutes
Ingredients:
- FOR THE PORK LOIN
- 2 pounds pork loin roast
- 2 tablespoons vegetable oil
- 2 teaspoons dried thyme
- 2 teaspoons dried crushed rosemary
- 1 teaspoon minced garlic
- ¾ teaspoon kosher salt
- FOR THE SCALLOPED POTATOES AND CAULIFLOWER
- 1 teaspoon vegetable oil
- ¾ pound Yukon Gold potatoes, peeled and very thinly sliced
- 1½ cups cauliflower florets
- ¼ teaspoon kosher salt
- ¼ teaspoon freshly ground black pepper
- 1 tablespoon very cold unsalted butter, grated
- 3 tablespoons all-purpose flour
- 1 cup whole milk
- 1 cup shredded Gruyère cheese

Directions:
1. To prep the pork loin: Coat the pork with the oil. Season with thyme, rosemary, garlic, and salt.
2. To prep the potatoes and cauliflower: Brush the bottom and sides of the Zone 2 basket with the oil. Add one-third of the potatoes to the bottom of the basket and arrange in a single layer. Top with ½ cup of cauliflower florets. Sprinkle a third of the salt and black pepper on top. Scatter one-third of the butter on top and sprinkle on 1 tablespoon of flour. Repeat this step twice more for a total of three layers.
3. Pour the milk over the layered potatoes and cauliflower; it should just cover the top layer. Top with the Gruyère.
4. To cook the pork and scalloped vegetables: Install a crisper plate in the Zone 1 basket. Place the pork loin in the basket and insert the basket in the unit. Insert the Zone 2 basket in the unit.
5. Select Zone 1, select AIR FRY, set the temperature to 390°F, and set the time to 50 minutes.
6. Select Zone 2, select BAKE, set the temperature to 350°F, and set the time to 45 minutes. Select SMART FINISH.
7. Press START/PAUSE to begin cooking.
8. When cooking is complete, the pork will be cooked through (an instant-read thermometer should read 145°F) and the potatoes and cauliflower will be tender.
9. Let the pork rest for at least 15 minutes before slicing and serving with the scalloped vegetables.

Nutrition:
- (Per serving) Calories: 439; Total fat: 25g; Saturated fat: 10g; Carbohydrates: 17g; Fiber: 1.5g; Protein: 37g; Sodium: 431mg

Pork Chops And Potatoes

Servings: 3
Cooking Time: 12 Minutes
Ingredients:
- 455g red potatoes
- Olive oil
- Salt and pepper
- 1 teaspoon garlic powder
- 1 teaspoon fresh rosemary, chopped
- 2 tablespoons brown sugar
- 1 tablespoon soy sauce
- 1 tablespoon Worcestershire sauce
- 1 teaspoon lemon juice
- 3 small pork chops

Directions:
1. Mix potatoes and pork chops with remaining ingredients in a bowl.
2. Divide the ingredients in the air fryer baskets.
3. Return the air fryer basket 1 to Zone 1, and basket 2 to Zone 2 of the Ninja Foodi 2-Basket Air Fryer.
4. Choose the "Air Fry" mode for Zone 1 at 400 degrees F and 12 minutes of cooking time.
5. Select the "MATCH COOK" option to copy the settings for Zone 2.
6. Initiate cooking by pressing the START/PAUSE BUTTON.
7. Flip the chops and toss potatoes once cooked halfway through.
8. Serve warm.

Panko Crusted Calf's Liver Strips

Servings: 4
Cooking Time: 23 To 25 Minutes
Ingredients:
- 450 g sliced calf's liver, cut into ½-inch wide strips
- 2 eggs
- 2 tablespoons milk
- 120 ml whole wheat flour
- 475 ml panko breadcrumbs
- Salt and ground black pepper, to taste
- Cooking spray

Directions:
1. Preheat the air fryer to 200°C and spritz with cooking spray.
2. Rub the calf's liver strips with salt and ground black pepper on a clean work surface.
3. Whisk the eggs with milk in a large bowl. Pour the flour in a shallow dish. Pour the panko on a separate shallow dish.
4. Dunk the liver strips in the flour, then in the egg mixture. Shake the excess off and roll the strips over the panko to coat well.
5. Arrange the liver strips in a single layer in the two preheated air fryer drawers and spritz with cooking spray.
6. Air fry for 5 minutes or until browned. Flip the strips halfway through.
7. Serve immediately.

Yogurt Lamb Chops

Servings:2
Cooking Time:20
Ingredients:
- 1½ cups plain Greek yogurt
- 1 lemon, juice only
- 1 teaspoon ground cumin
- 1 teaspoon ground coriander
- ¾ teaspoon ground turmeric
- ¼ teaspoon ground allspice
- 10 rib lamb chops (1–1¼ inches thick cut)
- 2 tablespoons olive oil, divided

Directions:
1. Take a bowl and add lamb chop along with listed ingredients.
2. Rub the lamb chops well.
3. and let it marinate in the refrigerator for 1 hour.
4. Afterward takeout the lamb chops from the refrigerator.
5. Layer parchment paper on top of the baskets of the air fryer.
6. Divide it between ninja air fryer baskets.
7. Set the time for zone 1 to 20 minutes at 400 degrees F.
8. Select the MATCH button for the zone 2 basket.
9. Hit start and then wait for the chop to be cooked.
10. Once the cooking is done, the cool sign will appear on display.
11. Take out the lamb chops and let the chops serve on plates.

Nutrition:
- (Per serving) Calories1973 | Fat90 g| Sodium228 mg | Carbs 109.2g | Fiber 1g | Sugar 77.5g | Protein 184g

Beef Kofta Kebab

Servings: 4
Cooking Time: 20 Minutes
Ingredients:
- 455g ground beef
- ¼ cup white onion, grated
- ¼ cup parsley, chopped
- 1 tablespoon mint, chopped
- 2 cloves garlic, minced
- 1 teaspoon salt
- ½ teaspoon cumin
- 1 teaspoon oregano
- ½ teaspoon garlic salt
- 1 egg

Directions:
1. Mix ground beef with onion, parsley, mint, garlic, cumin, oregano, garlic salt and egg in a bowl.
2. Take 3 tbsp-sized beef kebabs out of this mixture.
3. Place the kebabs in the air fryer baskets.
4. Return the air fryer basket 1 to Zone 1, and basket 2 to Zone 2 of the Ninja Foodi 2-Basket Air Fryer.
5. Choose the "Air Fry" mode for Zone 1 at 375 degrees F and 18 minutes of cooking time.
6. Select the "MATCH COOK" option to copy the settings for Zone 2.
7. Initiate cooking by pressing the START/PAUSE BUTTON.
8. Flip the kebabs once cooked halfway through.
9. Serve warm.

Fish And Seafood Recipes

Seasoned Tuna Steaks

Servings: 4
Cooking Time: 9 Minutes
Ingredients:
- 1 teaspoon garlic powder
- ½ teaspoon salt
- ¼ teaspoon dried thyme
- ¼ teaspoon dried oregano
- 4 tuna steaks
- 2 tablespoons olive oil
- 1 lemon, quartered

Directions:
1. Preheat the air fryer to 190°C.
2. In a small bowl, whisk together the garlic powder, salt, thyme, and oregano.
3. Coat the tuna steaks with olive oil. Season both sides of each steak with the seasoning blend. Place the steaks in a single layer in the two air fryer baskets.
4. Roast for 5 minutes, then flip and roast for an additional 3 to 4 minutes.

Bacon-wrapped Shrimp

Servings: 8
Cooking Time: 10 Minutes
Ingredients:
- 24 jumbo raw shrimp, deveined with tail on, fresh or thawed from frozen
- 8 slices bacon, cut into thirds
- 1 tablespoon olive oil
- 1 teaspoon paprika
- 1–2 cloves minced garlic
- 1 tablespoon finely chopped fresh parsley

Directions:
1. Combine the olive oil, paprika, garlic, and parsley in a small bowl.
2. If necessary, peel the raw shrimp, leaving the tails on.
3. Add the shrimp to the oil mixture. Toss to coat well.
4. Wrap a piece of bacon around the middle of each shrimp and place seam-side down on a small baking dish.
5. Refrigerate for 30 minutes before cooking.
6. Place a crisper plate in each drawer. Put the shrimp in a single layer in each drawer. Insert the drawers into the unit.
7. Select zone 1, then AIR FRY, then set the temperature to 360 degrees F/ 180 degrees C with a 10-minute timer. To match zone 2 settings to zone 1, choose MATCH. To begin, select START/STOP.
8. Remove the shrimp from the drawers when the cooking time is over.

Nutrition:
- (Per serving) Calories 479 | Fat 15.7g | Sodium 949mg | Carbs 0.6g | Fiber 0.1g | Sugar 0g | Protein 76.1g

Air Fryer Calamari

Servings: 4
Cooking Time: 7 Minutes
Ingredients:
- ½ cup all-purpose flour
- 1 large egg
- 59ml milk
- 2 cups panko bread crumbs
- 1 teaspoon sea salt
- 1 teaspoon black pepper
- 455g calamari rings
- nonstick cooking spray

Directions:
1. Beat egg with milk in a bowl.
2. Mix flour with black pepper and salt in a bowl.
3. Coat the calamari rings with the flour mixture then dip in the egg mixture and coat with the breadcrumbs.
4. Place the coated calamari in the air fryer baskets.
5. Return the air fryer basket 1 to Zone 1, and basket 2 to Zone 2 of the Ninja Foodi 2-Basket Air Fryer.
6. Choose the "Air Fry" mode for Zone 1 at 400 degrees F and 7 minutes of cooking time.
7. Select the "MATCH COOK" option to copy the settings for Zone 2.
8. Initiate cooking by pressing the START/PAUSE BUTTON.
9. Flip the calamari rings once cooked half way through.
10. Serve warm.

Nutrition:
- (Per serving) Calories 336 | Fat 6g | Sodium 181mg | Carbs 1.3g | Fiber 0.2g | Sugar 0.4g | Protein 69.2g

Shrimp Po'boys With Sweet Potato Fries

Servings: 4
Cooking Time: 30 Minutes

Ingredients:
- FOR THE SHRIMP PO'BOYS
- ½ cup buttermilk
- 1 tablespoon Louisiana-style hot sauce
- ¾ cup all-purpose flour
- ½ cup cornmeal
- ½ teaspoon kosher salt
- ½ teaspoon paprika
- ½ teaspoon garlic powder
- ½ teaspoon freshly ground black pepper
- 1 pound peeled medium shrimp, thawed if frozen
- Nonstock cooking spray
- ½ cup store-bought rémoulade sauce
- 4 French bread rolls, halved lengthwise
- ½ cup shredded lettuce
- 1 tomato, sliced
- FOR THE SWEET POTATO FRIES
- 2 medium sweet potatoes
- 2 teaspoons vegetable oil
- ¼ teaspoon garlic powder
- ¼ teaspoon paprika
- ¼ teaspoon kosher salt

Directions:
1. To prep the shrimp: In a medium bowl, combine the buttermilk and hot sauce. In a shallow bowl, combine the flour, cornmeal, salt, paprika, garlic powder, and black pepper.
2. Add the shrimp to the buttermilk and stir to coat. Remove the shrimp, letting the excess buttermilk drip off, then add to the cornmeal mixture to coat.
3. Spritz the breaded shrimp with cooking spray, then let sit for 10 minutes.
4. To prep the sweet potatoes: Peel the sweet potatoes and cut them lengthwise into ¼-inch-thick sticks (like shoestring fries).
5. In a large bowl, combine the sweet potatoes, oil, garlic powder, paprika, and salt. Toss to coat.
6. To cook the shrimp and fries: Install a crisper plate in each of the two baskets. Place the shrimp in the Zone 1 basket and insert the basket in the unit. Place the sweet potatoes in a single layer in the Zone 2 basket and insert the basket in the unit.
7. Select Zone 1, select AIR FRY, set the temperature to 390°F, and set the timer to 13 minutes.
8. Select Zone 2, select AIR FRY, set the temperature to 400°F, and set the timer to 30 minutes. Select SMART FINISH.
9. Press START/PAUSE to begin cooking.
10. When cooking is complete, the shrimp should be golden and cooked through and the sweet potato fries crisp.
11. Spread the rémoulade on the cut sides of the rolls. Divide the lettuce and tomato among the rolls, then top with the fried shrimp. Serve with the sweet potato fries on the side.

Nutrition:
- (Per serving) Calories: 669; Total fat: 22g; Saturated fat: 2g; Carbohydrates: 86g; Fiber: 3.5g; Protein: 33g; Sodium: 1,020mg

Crusted Tilapia

Servings: 4
Cooking Time: 17 Minutes

Ingredients:
- ¾ cup breadcrumbs
- 1 packet dry ranch-style dressing
- 2 ½ tablespoons vegetable oil
- 2 eggs beaten
- 4 tilapia fillets
- Herbs and chilies to garnish

Directions:
1. Thoroughly mix ranch dressing with panko in a bowl.
2. Whisk eggs in a shallow bowl.
3. Dip each fish fillet in the egg, then coat evenly with the panko mixture.
4. Set two coated fillets in each of the crisper plate.
5. Return the crisper plates to the Ninja Foodi Dual Zone Air Fryer.
6. Choose the Air Fry mode for Zone 1 and set the temperature to 390 degrees F and the time to 17 minutes
7. Select the "MATCH" button to copy the settings for Zone 2.
8. Initiate cooking by pressing the START/STOP button.
9. Serve warm with herbs and chilies.

Fish Tacos

Servings: 5
Cooking Time: 30 Minutes
Ingredients:
- 1 pound firm white fish such as cod, haddock, pollock, halibut, or walleye
- ¾ cup gluten-free flour blend
- 3 eggs
- 1 cup gluten-free panko breadcrumbs
- 1 teaspoon garlic powder
- 1 teaspoon onion powder
- 1 teaspoon cumin
- 1 teaspoon lemon pepper
- 1 teaspoon red chili flakes
- 1 teaspoon kosher salt, divided
- 1 teaspoon pepper, divided
- Cooking oil spray
- 1 package corn tortillas
- Toppings such as tomatoes, avocado, cabbage, radishes, jalapenos, salsa, or hot sauce (optional)

Directions:
1. Dry the fish with paper towels. (Make sure to thaw the fish if it's frozen.) Depending on the size of the fillets, cut the fish in half or thirds.
2. On both sides of the fish pieces, liberally season with salt and pepper.
3. Put the flour in a dish.
4. In a separate bowl, crack the eggs and whisk them together until well blended.
5. Put the panko breadcrumbs in another bowl. Add the garlic powder, onion powder, cumin, lemon pepper, and red chili flakes. Add salt and pepper to taste. Stir until everything is well blended.
6. Each piece of fish should be dipped in the flour, then the eggs, and finally in the breadcrumb mixture. Make sure that each piece is completely coated.
7. Put a crisper plate in each drawer. Arrange the fish pieces in a single layer in each drawer. Insert the drawers into the unit.
8. Select zone 1, then AIR FRY, then set the temperature to 360 degrees F/ 180 degrees C with a 20-minute timer. To match zone 2 settings to zone 1, choose MATCH. To begin, select START/STOP.
9. Remove the fish from the drawers after the timer has finished. Place the crispy fish on warmed tortillas.

Nutrition:
- (Per serving) Calories 534 | Fat 18g | Sodium 679mg | Carbs 63g | Fiber 8g | Sugar 3g | Protein 27g

Tuna-stuffed Quinoa Patties

Servings: 4
Cooking Time: 15 Minutes
Ingredients:
- 35 g quinoa
- 4 slices white bread with crusts removed
- 120 ml milk
- 3 eggs
- 280 g tuna packed in olive oil, drained
- 2 to 3 lemons
- Kosher or coarse sea salt, and pepper, to taste
- 150 g panko bread crumbs
- Vegetable oil, for spraying
- Lemon wedges, for serving

Directions:
1. Rinse the quinoa in a fine-mesh sieve until the water runs clear. Bring 1 liter of salted water to a boil. Add the quinoa, cover, and reduce heat to low. Simmer the quinoa covered until most of the water is absorbed and the quinoa is tender, 15 to 20 minutes. Drain and allow to cool to room temperature. Meanwhile, soak the bread in the milk.
2. Mix the drained quinoa with the soaked bread and 2 of the eggs in a large bowl and mix thoroughly. In a medium bowl, combine the tuna, the remaining egg, and the juice and zest of 1 of the lemons. Season well with salt and pepper. Spread the panko on a plate.
3. Scoop up approximately 60 g of the quinoa mixture and flatten into a patty. Place a heaping tablespoon of the tuna mixture in the center of the patty and close the quinoa around the tuna. Flatten the patty slightly to create an oval-shaped croquette. Dredge both sides of the croquette in the panko. Repeat with the remaining quinoa and tuna.
4. Spray the two air fryer baskets with oil to prevent sticking, and preheat the air fryer to 205°C. Arrange 4 or 5 of the croquettes in each basket, taking care to avoid overcrowding. Spray the tops of the croquettes with oil. Air fry for 8 minutes until the top side is browned and crispy. Carefully turn the croquettes over and spray the second side with oil. Air fry until the second side is browned and crispy, another 7 minutes.
5. Serve the croquetas warm with plenty of lemon wedges for spritzing.

Blackened Mahimahi With Honey-roasted Carrots

Servings: 4
Cooking Time: 30 Minutes
Ingredients:
- FOR THE MAHIMAHI
- 4 mahimahi fillets (4 ounces each)
- 1 tablespoon olive oil
- 1 tablespoon blackening seasoning
- Lemon wedges, for serving
- FOR THE CARROTS
- 1 pound carrots, peeled and cut into ½-inch rounds
- 2 teaspoons vegetable oil
- ½ teaspoon kosher salt
- ¼ teaspoon freshly ground black pepper
- 1 tablespoon salted butter, cut into small pieces
- 1 tablespoon honey
- 2 tablespoons chopped fresh parsley

Directions:
1. To prep the mahimahi: Brush both sides of the fish with the oil and sprinkle with the blackening seasoning.
2. To prep the carrots: In a large bowl, combine the carrots, oil, salt, and black pepper. Stir well to coat the carrots with the oil.
3. To cook the mahimahi and carrots: Install a crisper plate in each of the two baskets. Place the fish in the Zone 1 basket and insert the basket in the unit. Place the carrots in the Zone 2 basket and insert the basket in the unit.
4. Select Zone 1, select AIR FRY, set the temperature to 380°F, and set the timer to 14 minutes.
5. Select Zone 2, select ROAST, set the temperature to 400°F, and set the timer to 30 minutes. Select SMART FINISH.
6. Press START/PAUSE to begin cooking.
7. When the Zone 2 timer reads 15 minutes, press START/PAUSE. Remove the basket and scatter the butter over the carrots, then drizzle them with the honey. Reinsert the basket and press START/PAUSE to resume cooking.
8. When cooking is complete, the fish should be cooked through and the carrots soft.
9. Stir the parsley into the carrots. Serve the fish with lemon wedges.

Nutrition:
- (Per serving) Calories: 235; Total fat: 9.5g; Saturated fat: 3g; Carbohydrates: 15g; Fiber: 3g; Protein: 22g; Sodium: 672mg

Steamed Cod With Garlic And Swiss Chard

Servings: 4
Cooking Time: 12 Minutes
Ingredients:
- 1 teaspoon salt
- ½ teaspoon dried oregano
- ½ teaspoon dried thyme
- ½ teaspoon garlic powder
- 4 cod fillets
- ½ white onion, thinly sliced
- 135 g Swiss chard, washed, stemmed, and torn into pieces
- 60 ml olive oil
- 1 lemon, quartered

Directions:
1. Preheat the air fryer to 192°C.
2. In a small bowl, whisk together the salt, oregano, thyme, and garlic powder.
3. Tear off four pieces of aluminum foil, with each sheet being large enough to envelop one cod fillet and a quarter of the vegetables.
4. Place a cod fillet in the middle of each sheet of foil, then sprinkle on all sides with the spice mixture.
5. In each foil packet, place a quarter of the onion slices and 30 g Swiss chard, then drizzle 1 tablespoon olive oil and squeeze ¼ lemon over the contents of each foil packet.
6. Fold and seal the sides of the foil packets and then place them into the two air fryer drawers. Steam for 12 minutes.
7. Remove from the drawers, and carefully open each packet to avoid a steam burn.

Parmesan Mackerel With Coriander And Garlic Butter Prawns Scampi

Servings: 6
Cooking Time: 8 Minutes

Ingredients:
- Parmesan Mackerel with Coriander:
- 340 g mackerel fillet
- 60 g Parmesan, grated
- 1 teaspoon ground coriander
- 1 tablespoon olive oil
- Garlic Butter Prawns Scampi:
- Sauce:
- 60 g unsalted butter
- 2 tablespoons fish stock or chicken broth
- 2 cloves garlic, minced
- 2 tablespoons chopped fresh basil leaves
- 1 tablespoon lemon juice
- 1 tablespoon chopped fresh parsley, plus more for garnish
- 1 teaspoon red pepper flakes
- Prawns:
- 455 g large prawns, peeled and deveined, tails removed
- Fresh basil sprigs, for garnish

Directions:
1. Make the Parmesan Mackerel with Coriander :
2. Sprinkle the mackerel fillet with olive oil and put it in the zone 1 air fryer drawer.
3. Top the fish with ground coriander and Parmesan.
4. Cook the fish at 200°C for 7 minutes.
5. Make the Garlic Butter Prawns Scampi :
6. Preheat the zone 2 air fryer drawer to 176°C.
7. Put all the ingredients for the sauce in a baking pan and stir to incorporate.
8. Transfer the baking pan to the zone 2 air fryer drawer and air fry for 3 minutes, or until the sauce is heated through.
9. Once done, add the prawns to the baking pan, flipping to coat in the sauce.
10. Return to the air fryer and cook for another 5 minutes, or until the prawns are pink and opaque. Stir the prawns twice during cooking.
11. Serve garnished with the parsley and basil sprigs.

Salmon Fritters With Courgette & Cajun And Lemon Pepper Cod

Servings: 6
Cooking Time: 12 Minutes

Ingredients:
- Salmon Fritters with Courgette:
- 2 tablespoons almond flour
- 1 courgette, grated
- 1 egg, beaten
- 170 g salmon fillet, diced
- 1 teaspoon avocado oil
- ½ teaspoon ground black pepper
- Cajun and Lemon Pepper Cod:
- 1 tablespoon Cajun seasoning
- 1 teaspoon salt
- ½ teaspoon lemon pepper
- ½ teaspoon freshly ground black pepper
- 2 cod fillets, 230 g each, cut to fit into the air fryer basket
- Cooking spray
- 2 tablespoons unsalted butter, melted
- 1 lemon, cut into 4 wedges

Directions:
1. Make the Salmon Fritters with Courgette :
2. Mix almond flour with courgette, egg, salmon, and ground black pepper.
3. Then make the fritters from the salmon mixture.
4. Sprinkle the zone 1 air fryer basket with avocado oil and put the fritters inside.
5. Cook the fritters at 190°C for 6 minutes per side.
6. Make the Cajun and Lemon Pepper Cod :
7. Preheat the air fryer to 180°C. Spritz the zone 2 air fryer basket with cooking spray.
8. Thoroughly combine the Cajun seasoning, salt, lemon pepper, and black pepper in a small bowl. Rub this mixture all over the cod fillets until completely coated.
9. Put the fillets in the air fryer basket and brush the melted butter over both sides of each fillet.
10. Bake in the preheated air fryer for 12 minutes, flipping the fillets halfway through, or until the fish flakes easily with a fork.
11. Remove the fillets from the basket and serve with fresh lemon wedges.

Shrimp With Lemon And Pepper

Servings: 4
Cooking Time: 8 Minutes
Ingredients:
- 455g raw shrimp, peeled and deveined
- 118ml olive oil
- 2 tablespoons lemon juice
- 1 teaspoon black pepper
- ½ teaspoon salt

Directions:
1. Toss shrimp with black pepper, salt, lemon juice and oil in a bowl.
2. Divide the shrimp into the Ninja Foodi 2 Baskets Air Fryer baskets.
3. Return the air fryer basket 1 to Zone 1, and basket 2 to Zone 2 of the Ninja Foodi 2-Basket Air Fryer.
4. Choose the "Air Fry" mode for Zone 1 at 350 degrees F and 8 minutes of cooking time.
5. Select the "MATCH COOK" option to copy the settings for Zone 2.
6. Initiate cooking by pressing the START/PAUSE BUTTON.
7. Serve warm.

Nutrition:
- (Per serving) Calories 257 | Fat 10.4g | Sodium 431mg | Carbs 20g | Fiber 0g | Sugar 1.6g | Protein 21g

Healthy Lobster Cakes

Servings: 6
Cooking Time: 12 Minutes
Ingredients:
- 1 egg
- 145g cooked lobster meat
- 60g butter, melted
- 1 tbsp Cajun seasoning
- 50g breadcrumbs
- Pepper
- Salt

Directions:
1. In a shallow dish, add breadcrumbs, pepper, and salt.
2. In a bowl, mix lobster meat, Cajun seasoning, egg, and butter until well combined.
3. Make patties from the lobster meat mixture and coat with breadcrumbs.
4. Insert a crisper plate in the Ninja Foodi air fryer baskets.
5. Place the coated patties in both baskets.
6. Select zone 1, then select "bake" mode and set the temperature to 390 degrees F for 12 minutes. Press "match" to match zone 2 settings to zone 1. Press "start/stop" to begin.

Nutrition:
- (Per serving) Calories 119 | Fat 7.2g | Sodium 287mg | Carbs 6.6g | Fiber 0.4g | Sugar 0.6g | Protein 6.8g

Savory Salmon Fillets

Servings: 4
Cooking Time: 17 Minutes
Ingredients:
- 4 (6-oz) salmon fillets
- Salt, to taste
- Black pepper, to taste
- 4 teaspoons olive oil
- 4 tablespoons wholegrain mustard
- 2 tablespoons packed brown sugar
- 2 garlic cloves, minced
- 1 teaspoon thyme leaves

Directions:
1. Rub the salmon with salt and black pepper first.
2. Whisk oil with sugar, thyme, garlic, and mustard in a small bowl.
3. Place two salmon fillets in each of the crisper plate and brush the thyme mixture on top of each fillet.
4. Return the crisper plates to the Ninja Foodi Dual Zone Air Fryer.
5. Choose the Air Fry mode for Zone 1 and set the temperature to 390 degrees F and the time to 17 minutes|
6. Select the "MATCH" button to copy the settings for Zone 2.
7. Initiate cooking by pressing the START/STOP button.
8. Serve warm and fresh.

Thai Prawn Skewers And Lemon-tarragon Fish En Papillote

Servings: 5
Cooking Time: 15 Minutes
Ingredients:
- Lemon-Tarragon Fish en Papillote:
- Salt and pepper, to taste
- 340 g extra-large prawns, peeled and deveined
- 1 tablespoon vegetable oil
- 1 teaspoon honey
- ½ teaspoon grated lime zest plus 1 tablespoon juice, plus lime wedges for serving
- 6 (6-inch) wooden skewers
- 3 tablespoons creamy peanut butter
- 3 tablespoons hot tap water
- 1 tablespoon chopped fresh coriander
- 1 teaspoon fish sauce
- Lemon-Tarragon Fish en Papillote:
- 2 tablespoons salted butter, melted
- 1 tablespoon fresh lemon juice
- ½ teaspoon dried tarragon, crushed, or 2 sprigs fresh tarragon
- 1 teaspoon kosher or coarse sea salt
- 85 g julienned carrots
- 435 g julienned fennel, or 1 stalk julienned celery
- 75 g thinly sliced red bell pepper
- 2 cod fillets, 170 g each, thawed if frozen
- Vegetable oil spray
- ½ teaspoon black pepper

Directions:
1. Make the Lemon-Tarragon Fish en Papillote :
2. Preheat the air fryer to 204°C.
3. Dissolve 2 tablespoons salt in 1 litre cold water in a large container. Add prawns, cover, and refrigerate for 15 minutes.
4. Remove prawns from brine and pat dry with paper towels. Whisk oil, honey, lime zest, and ¼ teaspoon pepper together in a large bowl. Add prawns and toss to coat. Thread prawns onto skewers, leaving about ¼ inch between each prawns .
5. Arrange 3 skewers in the zone 1 air fryer drawer, parallel to each other and spaced evenly apart. Arrange remaining 3 skewers on top, perpendicular to the bottom layer. Air fry until prawns are opaque throughout, 6 to 8 minutes, flipping and rotating skewers halfway through cooking.
6. Whisk peanut butter, hot tap water, lime juice, coriander, and fish sauce together in a bowl until smooth. Serve skewers with peanut dipping sauce and lime wedges.
7. Make the Lemon-Tarragon Fish en Papillote :
8. In a medium bowl, combine the butter, lemon juice, tarragon, and ½ teaspoon of the salt. Whisk well until you get a creamy sauce. Add the carrots, fennel, and bell pepper and toss to combine; set aside.
9. Cut two squares of baking paper each large enough to hold one fillet and half the vegetables. Spray the fillets with vegetable oil spray. Season both sides with the remaining ½ teaspoon salt and the black pepper.
10. Lay one fillet down on each baking paper square. Top each with half the vegetables. Pour any remaining sauce over the vegetables.
11. Fold over the baking paper and crimp the sides in small, tight folds to hold the fish, vegetables, and sauce securely inside the packet. Place the packets in the zone 2 air fryer drawer. Set the air fryer to 176°C for 15 minutes.
12. Transfer each packet to a plate. Cut open with scissors just before serving .

Lemon-pepper Trout

Servings: 4
Cooking Time: 15 Minutes
Ingredients:
- 4 trout fillets
- 2 tablespoons olive oil
- ½ teaspoon salt
- 1 teaspoon black pepper
- 2 garlic cloves, sliced
- 1 lemon, sliced, plus additional wedges for serving

Directions:
1. Preheat the air fryer to 190°C.
2. Brush each fillet with olive oil on both sides and season with salt and pepper. Place the fillets in an even layer in the two air fryer baskets.
3. Place the sliced garlic over the tops of the trout fillets, then top the garlic with lemon slices and roast for 12 to 15 minutes, or until it has reached an internal temperature of 65°C.
4. Serve with fresh lemon wedges.

Prawn Creole Casserole And Garlic Lemon Scallops

Servings: 8
Cooking Time: 25 Minutes
Ingredients:
- Prawn Creole Casserole:
- 360 g prawns, peeled and deveined
- 50 g chopped celery
- 50 g chopped onion
- 50 g chopped green bell pepper
- 2 large eggs, beaten
- 240 ml single cream
- 1 tablespoon butter, melted
- 1 tablespoon cornflour
- 1 teaspoon Creole seasoning
- ¾ teaspoon salt
- ½ teaspoon freshly ground black pepper
- 120 g shredded Cheddar cheese
- Cooking spray
- Garlic Lemon Scallops:
- 4 tablespoons salted butter, melted
- 4 teaspoons peeled and finely minced garlic
- ½ small lemon, zested and juiced
- 8 sea scallops, 30 g each, cleaned and patted dry
- ¼ teaspoon salt
- ¼ teaspoon ground black pepper

Directions:
1. Make the Prawn Creole Casserole :
2. In a medium bowl, stir together the prawns, celery, onion, and green pepper.
3. In another medium bowl, whisk the eggs, single cream, butter, cornflour, Creole seasoning, salt, and pepper until blended. Stir the egg mixture into the prawn mixture. Add the cheese and stir to combine.
4. Preheat the air fryer to 150°C. Spritz a baking pan with oil.
5. Transfer the prawn mixture to the prepared pan and place it in the zone 1 air fryer drawer.
6. Bake for 25 minutes, stirring every 10 minutes, until a knife inserted into the center comes out clean.
7. Serve immediately.
8. Make the Garlic Lemon Scallops :
9. In a small bowl, mix butter, garlic, lemon zest, and lemon juice. Place scallops in an ungreased round nonstick baking dish. Pour butter mixture over scallops, then sprinkle with salt and pepper.
10. Place dish into the zone 2 air fryer drawer. Adjust the temperature to 182°C and bake for 10 minutes. Scallops will be opaque and firm, and have an internal temperature of 56°C when done. Serve warm.

Tilapia Sandwiches With Tartar Sauce

Servings: 4
Cooking Time: 17 Minutes
Ingredients:
- 160 g mayonnaise
- 2 tablespoons dried minced onion
- 1 dill pickle spear, finely chopped
- 2 teaspoons pickle juice
- ¼ teaspoon salt
- ⅛ teaspoon freshly ground black pepper
- 40 g plain flour
- 1 egg, lightly beaten
- 200 g panko bread crumbs
- 2 teaspoons lemon pepper
- 4 (170 g) tilapia fillets
- Olive oil spray
- 4 soft sub rolls
- 4 lettuce leaves

Directions:
1. To make the tartar sauce, in a small bowl, whisk the mayonnaise, dried onion, pickle, pickle juice, salt, and pepper until blended. Refrigerate while you make the fish.
2. Scoop the flour onto a plate; set aside.
3. Put the beaten egg in a medium shallow bowl.
4. On another plate, stir together the panko and lemon pepper.
5. Preheat the air fryer to 205°C.
6. Dredge the tilapia fillets in the flour, in the egg, and press into the panko mixture to coat.
7. Once the unit is preheated, spray the zone 1 basket with olive oil and place a baking paper liner into the basket. Place the prepared fillets on the liner in a single layer. Lightly spray the fillets with olive oil.
8. cook for 8 minutes, remove the basket, carefully flip the fillets, and spray them with more olive oil. Reinsert the basket to resume cooking.
9. When the cooking is complete, the fillets should be golden and crispy and a food thermometer should register 65°C. Place each cooked fillet in a sub roll, top with a little bit of tartar sauce and lettuce, and serve.

Herb Lemon Mussels

Servings: 6
Cooking Time: 10 Minutes
Ingredients:
- 1kg mussels, steamed & half shell
- 1 tbsp thyme, chopped
- 1 tbsp parsley, chopped
- 1 tsp dried parsley
- 1 tsp garlic, minced
- 60ml olive oil
- 45ml lemon juice
- Pepper
- Salt

Directions:
1. In a bowl, mix mussels with the remaining ingredients.
2. Insert a crisper plate in the Ninja Foodi air fryer baskets.
3. Add the mussels to both baskets.
4. Select zone 1 then select "air fry" mode and set the temperature to 360 degrees F for 10 minutes. Press "match" to match zone 2 settings to zone 1. Press "start/stop" to begin.

Nutrition:
- (Per serving) Calories 206 | Fat 11.9g |Sodium 462mg | Carbs 6.3g | Fiber 0.3g | Sugar 0.2g | Protein 18.2g

Seafood Shrimp Omelet

Servings:2
Cooking Time:15
Ingredients:
- 6 large shrimp, shells removed and chopped
- 6 eggs, beaten
- ½ tablespoon of butter, melted
- 2 tablespoons green onions, sliced
- 1/3 cup of mushrooms, chopped
- 1 pinch paprika
- Salt and black pepper, to taste
- Oil spray, for greasing

Directions:
1. In a large bowl whisk the eggs and add chopped shrimp, butter, green onions, mushrooms, paprika, salt, and black pepper.
2. Take two cake pans that fit inside the air fryer and grease them with oil spray.
3. Pour the egg mixture between the cake pans and place it in two baskets of the air fryer.
4. Turn on the BAKE function of zone 1, and let it cook for 15 minutes at 320 degrees F.
5. Select the MATCH button to match the cooking time for the zone 2 basket.
6. Once the cooking cycle completes, take out, and serve hot.

Nutrition:
- (Per serving) Calories 300 | Fat 17.5g| Sodium 368mg | Carbs 2.9g | Fiber 0.3g | Sugar1.4 g | Protein32.2 g

Delicious Haddock

Servings: 4
Cooking Time: 10 Minutes
Ingredients:
- 1 egg
- 455g haddock fillets
- 1 tsp seafood seasoning
- 136g flour
- 15ml olive oil
- 119g breadcrumbs
- Pepper
- Salt

Directions:
1. In a shallow dish, whisk egg. Add flour to a plate.
2. In a separate shallow dish, mix breadcrumbs, pepper, seafood seasoning, and salt.
3. Brush fish fillets with oil.
4. Coat each fish fillet with flour, then dip in egg and finally coat with breadcrumbs.
5. Insert a crisper plate in the Ninja Foodi air fryer baskets.
6. Place coated fish fillets in both baskets.
7. Select zone 1, then select "air fry" mode and set the temperature to 360 degrees F for 10 minutes. Press "match" to match zone 2 settings to zone 1. Press "start/stop" to begin.

Nutrition:
- (Per serving) Calories 393 | Fat 7.4g |Sodium 351mg | Carbs 43.4g | Fiber 2.1g | Sugar 1.8g | Protein 35.7g

Lemony Prawns And Courgette

Servings: 4
Cooking Time: 7 To 8 Minutes
Ingredients:
- 570 g extra-large raw prawns, peeled and deveined
- 2 medium courgettes (about 230 g each), halved lengthwise and cut into ½-inch-thick slices
- 1½ tablespoons olive oil
- ½ teaspoon garlic salt
- 1½ teaspoons dried oregano
- ⅛ teaspoon crushed red pepper flakes (optional)
- Juice of ½ lemon
- 1 tablespoon chopped fresh mint
- 1 tablespoon chopped fresh dill

Directions:
1. Preheat the air fryer to 176°C.
2. In a large bowl, combine the prawns, courgette, oil, garlic salt, oregano, and pepper flakes and toss to coat.
3. Arrange a single layer of the prawns and courgette in the two air fryer drawers. Air fry for 7 to 8 minutes, shaking the drawer halfway, until the courgette is golden and the prawns are cooked through.
4. Transfer to a serving dish and tent with foil while you air fry the remaining prawns and courgette.
5. Top with the lemon juice, mint, and dill and serve.

Tuna Patties

Servings: 6
Cooking Time: 10 Minutes
Ingredients:
- For the tuna patties:
- 1 tablespoon extra-virgin olive oil
- 1 tablespoon butter
- ½ cup chopped onion
- ½ red bell pepper, chopped
- 1 teaspoon minced garlic
- 2 (7-ounce) cans or 3 (5-ounce) cans albacore tuna fish in water, drained
- 1 tablespoon lime juice
- 1 celery stalk, chopped
- ¼ cup chopped fresh parsley
- 3 tablespoons grated parmesan cheese
- ½ teaspoon dried oregano
- ¼ teaspoon salt
- Black pepper, to taste
- 1 teaspoon sriracha
- ½ cup panko crumbs
- 2 whisked eggs
- For the crumb coating:
- ½ cup panko crumbs
- ¼ cup parmesan cheese
- Non-stick spray

Directions:
1. In a skillet, heat the oil and butter over medium-high heat.
2. Sauté the onions, red bell pepper, and garlic for 5 to 7 minutes.
3. Drain the tuna from the cans thoroughly. Put the tuna in a large mixing bowl. Add the lime juice.
4. Add the sautéed vegetables to the mixing bowl.
5. Add the celery, parsley, and cheese. Combine well.
6. Add the oregano, salt, and pepper to taste. Mix well.
7. Add a dash of sriracha for a spicy kick and mix well.
8. Add the panko crumbs and mix well.
9. Mix in the eggs until the mixture is well combined. You can add an extra egg if necessary, but the tuna is usually wet enough that it isn't required. Form 6 patties from the mixture.
10. Refrigerate for 30 to 60 minutes (or even overnight).
11. Remove from refrigerator and coat with a mixture of the ½ cup of panko crumbs and ¼ cup of parmesan cheese.
12. Spray the tops of the coated patties with some non-stick cooking spray.
13. Place a crisper place in each drawer. Put 3 patties in each drawer. Insert the drawers into the unit.
14. Select zone 1, then AIR FRY, then set the temperature to 390 degrees F/ 200 degrees C with a 10-minute timer. To match zone 2 settings to zone 1, choose MATCH. To begin, select START/STOP.
15. Remove and garnish with chopped parsley.

Nutrition:
- (Per serving) Calories 381 | Fat 16g | Sodium 1007mg | Carbs 23g | Fiber 2g | Sugar 4g | Protein 38g

Snapper With Fruit

Servings: 4
Cooking Time: 9 To 13 Minutes
Ingredients:
- 4 red snapper fillets, 100 g each
- 2 teaspoons olive oil
- 3 nectarines, halved and pitted
- 3 plums, halved and pitted
- 150 g red grapes
- 1 tablespoon freshly squeezed lemon juice
- 1 tablespoon honey
- ½ teaspoon dried thyme

Directions:
1. Put the red snapper in the two air fryer baskets and drizzle with the olive oil. Air fry at 200°C for 4 minutes.
2. Remove the baskets and add the nectarines and plums. Scatter the grapes over all.
3. Drizzle with the lemon juice and honey and sprinkle with the thyme.
4. Return the baskets to the air fryer and air fry for 5 to 9 minutes more, or until the fish flakes when tested with a fork and the fruit is tender. Serve immediately.

Italian Baked Cod

Servings: 4
Cooking Time: 12 Minutes
Ingredients:
- 4 cod fillets, 170 g each
- 2 tablespoons salted butter, melted
- 1 teaspoon Italian seasoning
- ¼ teaspoon salt
- 120 ml tomato-based pasta sauce

Directions:
1. Place cod into an ungreased round nonstick baking dish. Pour butter over cod and sprinkle with Italian seasoning and salt. Top with pasta sauce.
2. Place dish into the two air fryer drawers. Adjust the temperature to 176°C and bake for 12 minutes. Fillets will be lightly browned, easily flake, and have an internal temperature of at least 64°C when done. Serve warm.

Breaded Scallops

Servings: 4
Cooking Time: 12 Minutes
Ingredients:
- ½ cup crushed buttery crackers
- ½ teaspoon garlic powder
- ½ teaspoon seafood seasoning
- 2 tablespoons butter, melted
- 1 pound sea scallops patted dry
- cooking spray

Directions:
1. Mix cracker crumbs, garlic powder, and seafood seasoning in a shallow bowl. Spread melted butter in another shallow bowl.
2. Dip each scallop in the melted butter and then roll in the breading to coat well.
3. Grease each Air fryer basket with cooking spray and place half of the scallops in each.
4. Return the crisper plate to the Ninja Foodi Dual Zone Air Fryer.
5. Select the Air Fry mode for Zone 1 and set the temperature to 390 degrees F and the time to 12 minutes
6. Press the "MATCH" button to copy the settings for Zone 2.
7. Initiate cooking by pressing the START/STOP button.
8. Flip the scallops with a spatula after 4 minutes and resume cooking.
9. Serve warm.

Tender Juicy Honey Glazed Salmon

Servings: 4
Cooking Time: 10 Minutes
Ingredients:
- 4 salmon fillets
- 1 tbsp honey
- 1/2 tsp red chili flakes, crushed
- 1 tsp sesame seeds, toasted
- 1 1/2 tsp olive oil
- 1 tbsp coconut aminos
- Pepper
- Salt

Directions:
1. Place salmon fillets into the bowl. In a small bowl, mix coconut aminos, oil, pepper, and salt and pour over fish fillets. Mix well.
2. Cover bowl and place in the refrigerator for 20 minutes.
3. Preheat the air fryer to 400 F.
4. Place marinated salmon fillets into the air fryer basket and cook for 8 minutes.
5. Brush fish fillets with honey and sprinkle with chili flakes and sesame seeds and cook for 2 minutes more.
6. Serve and enjoy.

Fried Tilapia

Servings: 4
Cooking Time: 20 Minutes
Ingredients:
- 4 fresh tilapia fillets, approximately 6 ounces each
- 2 teaspoons olive oil
- 2 teaspoons chopped fresh chives
- 2 teaspoons chopped fresh parsley
- 1 teaspoon minced garlic
- Freshly ground pepper, to taste
- Salt to taste

Directions:
1. Pat the tilapia fillets dry with a paper towel.
2. Stir together the olive oil, chives, parsley, garlic, salt, and pepper in a small bowl.
3. Brush the mixture over the top of the tilapia fillets.
4. Place a crisper plate in each drawer. Add the fillets in a single layer to each drawer. Insert the drawers into the unit.
5. Select zone 1, then AIR FRY, then set the temperature to 360 degrees F/ 180 degrees C with a 20-minute timer. To match zone 2 settings to zone 1, choose MATCH. To begin, select START/STOP.
6. Remove the tilapia fillets from the drawers after the timer has finished.

Nutrition:
- (Per serving) Calories 140 | Fat 5.7g | Sodium 125mg | Carbs 1.5g | Fiber 0.4g | Sugar 0g | Protein 21.7g

Salmon Patties

Servings: 8
Cooking Time: 18 Minutes
Ingredients:
- 1 lb. fresh Atlantic salmon side
- ¼ cup avocado, mashed
- ¼ cup cilantro, diced
- 1 ½ teaspoons yellow curry powder
- ½ teaspoons sea salt
- ¼ cup, 4 teaspoons tapioca starch
- 2 brown eggs
- ½ cup coconut flakes
- Coconut oil, melted, for brushing
- For the greens:
- 2 teaspoons organic coconut oil, melted
- 6 cups arugula & spinach mix, tightly packed
- Pinch of sea salt

Directions:
1. Remove the fish skin and dice the flesh.
2. Place in a large bowl. Add cilantro, avocado, salt, and curry powder mix gently.
3. Add tapioca starch and mix well again.
4. Make 8 salmon patties out of this mixture, about a half-inch thick.
5. Place them on a baking sheet lined with wax paper and freeze them for 20 minutes|
6. Place ¼ cup tapioca starch and coconut flakes on a flat plate.
7. Dip the patties in the whisked egg, then coat the frozen patties in the starch and flakes.
8. Place half of the patties in each of the crisper plate and spray them with cooking oil
9. Return the crisper plate to the Ninja Foodi Dual Zone Air Fryer.
10. Choose the Air Fry mode for Zone 1 and set the temperature to 390 degrees F and the time to 17 minutes|
11. Select the "MATCH" button to copy the settings for Zone 2.
12. Initiate cooking by pressing the START/STOP button.
13. Flip the patties once cooked halfway through, then resume cooking.
14. Sauté arugula with spinach in coconut oil in a pan for 30 seconds.
15. Serve the patties with sautéed greens mixture

Quick Easy Salmon

Servings: 4
Cooking Time: 8 Minutes
Ingredients:
- 4 salmon fillets
- 1/2 tsp smoked paprika
- 1 tsp garlic powder
- 1 tbsp olive oil
- Pepper
- Salt

Directions:
1. Preheat the air fryer to 400 F.
2. Brush salmon fillets with oil and sprinkle with smoked paprika, garlic powder, pepper, and salt.
3. Place salmon fillets into the air fryer basket and cook for 8 minutes.
4. Serve and enjoy.

Fish Sandwich

Servings: 4
Cooking Time: 22 Minutes
Ingredients:
- 4 small cod fillets, skinless
- Salt and black pepper, to taste
- 2 tablespoons flour
- ¼ cup dried breadcrumbs
- Spray oil
- 9 ounces of frozen peas
- 1 tablespoon creme fraiche
- 12 capers
- 1 squeeze of lemon juice
- 4 bread rolls, cut in halve

Directions:
1. First, coat the cod fillets with flour, salt, and black pepper.
2. Then coat the fish with breadcrumbs.
3. Divide the coated codfish in the two crisper plates and spray them with cooking spray.
4. Return the crisper plate to the Ninja Foodi Dual Zone Air Fryer.
5. Choose the Air Fry mode for Zone 1 and set the temperature to 390 degrees F and the time to 17 minutes|
6. Select the "MATCH" button to copy the settings for Zone 2.
7. Initiate cooking by pressing the START/STOP button.
8. Meanwhile, boil peas in hot water for 5 minutes until soft.
9. Then drain the peas and transfer them to the blender.
10. Add capers, lemon juice, and crème fraiche to the blender.
11. Blend until it makes a smooth mixture.
12. Spread the peas crème mixture on top of 2 lower halves of the bread roll, and place the fish fillets on it.
13. Place the remaining bread slices on top.
14. Serve fresh.

Garlic Shrimp With Pasta Alfredo

Servings: 4
Cooking Time: 40 Minutes
Ingredients:
- FOR THE GARLIC SHRIMP
- 1 pound peeled small shrimp, thawed if frozen
- 1 tablespoon olive oil
- 1 tablespoon minced garlic
- ¼ teaspoon sea salt
- ¼ cup chopped fresh parsley
- FOR THE PASTA ALFREDO
- 8 ounces no-boil lasagna noodles
- 2 cups whole milk
- ¼ cup heavy (whipping) cream
- 2 tablespoons unsalted butter, cut into small pieces
- 1 tablespoon minced garlic
- ½ teaspoon kosher salt
- ¼ teaspoon freshly ground black pepper
- ½ cup grated Parmesan cheese

Directions:
1. To prep the garlic shrimp: In a large bowl, combine the shrimp, oil, garlic, and salt.
2. To prep the pasta alfredo: Break the lasagna noodles into 2-inch pieces. Add the milk to the Zone 2 basket, then add the noodles, cream, butter, garlic, salt, and black pepper. Stir well and ensure the pasta is fully submerged in the liquid.
3. To cook the shrimp and pasta: Install a crisper plate in the Zone 1 basket. Place the shrimp in the basket and insert the basket in the unit. Insert the Zone 2 basket in the unit.
4. Select Zone 1, select AIR FRY, set the temperature to 390°F, and set the timer to 13 minutes.
5. Select Zone 2, select BAKE, set the temperature to 360°F, and set the timer to 40 minutes. Select SMART FINISH.
6. Press START/PAUSE to begin cooking.
7. When the Zone 2 timer reads 20 minutes, press START/PAUSE. Remove the basket and stir the pasta. Reinsert the basket and press START/PAUSE to resume cooking.
8. When cooking is complete, the shrimp will be cooked through and the pasta tender.
9. Transfer the pasta to a serving dish and stir in the Parmesan. Top with the shrimp and parsley.

Nutrition:
- (Per serving) Calories: 542; Total fat: 23g; Saturated fat: 11g; Carbohydrates: 52g; Fiber: 2g; Protein: 34g; Sodium: 643mg

Brown Sugar Garlic Salmon

Servings: 4
Cooking Time: 10 Minutes
Ingredients:
- 455g salmon
- Salt and black pepper, to taste
- 2 tablespoons brown sugar
- 1 teaspoon chili powder
- ½ teaspoon paprika
- 1 teaspoon Italian seasoning
- 1 teaspoon garlic powder

Directions:
1. Mix brown sugar with garlic powder, Italian seasoning, paprika, and chili powder in a bowl.
2. Rub this mixture over the salmon along with black pepper and salt.
3. Place the salmon in the air fryer baskets.
4. Return the air fryer basket 1 to Zone 1, and basket 2 to Zone 2 of the Ninja Foodi 2-Basket Air Fryer.
5. Choose the "Air Fry" mode for Zone 1 and set the temperature to 400 degrees F and 10 minutes of cooking time.
6. Select the "MATCH COOK" option to copy the settings for Zone 2.
7. Initiate cooking by pressing the START/PAUSE BUTTON.
8. Flip the salmon once cooked halfway through.
9. Serve warm.

Nutrition:
- (Per serving) Calories 275 | Fat 1.4g |Sodium 582mg | Carbs 31.5g | Fiber 1.1g | Sugar 0.1g | Protein 29.8g

Roasted Halibut Steaks With Parsley

Servings: 4
Cooking Time: 10 Minutes
Ingredients:
- 455 g halibut steaks
- 60 ml vegetable oil
- 2½ tablespoons Worcester sauce
- 2 tablespoons honey
- 2 tablespoons vermouth or white wine vinegar
- 1 tablespoon freshly squeezed lemon juice
- 1 tablespoon fresh parsley leaves, coarsely chopped
- Salt and pepper, to taste
- 1 teaspoon dried basil

Directions:
1. Preheat the air fryer to 200°C.
2. Put all the ingredients in a large mixing dish and gently stir until the fish is coated evenly.
3. Transfer the fish to the zone 1 air fryer drawer and roast for 10 minutes, flipping the fish halfway through, or until the fish reaches an internal temperature of at least 64°C on a meat thermometer.
4. Let the fish cool for 5 minutes and serve.

Cajun Catfish Cakes With Cheese

Servings: 4
Cooking Time: 35 Minutes
Ingredients:
- 2 catfish fillets
- 85 g butter
- 150 g shredded Parmesan cheese
- 150 g shredded Swiss cheese
- 120 ml buttermilk
- 1 teaspoon baking powder
- 1 teaspoon baking soda
- 1 teaspoon Cajun seasoning

Directions:
1. Bring a pot of salted water to a boil. Add the catfish fillets to the boiling water and let them boil for 5 minutes until they become opaque.
2. Remove the fillets from the pot to a mixing bowl and flake them into small pieces with a fork.
3. Add the remaining ingredients to the bowl of fish and stir until well incorporated.
4. Divide the fish mixture into 12 equal portions and shape each portion into a patty.
5. Preheat the air fryer to 190°C.
6. Arrange the patties in the two air fryer baskets and air fry for 15 minutes until golden brown and cooked through. Flip the patties halfway through the cooking time.
7. Let the patties sit for 5 minutes and serve.

Crispy Catfish

Servings: 4
Cooking Time: 17 Minutes
Ingredients:
- 4 catfish fillets
- ¼ cup Louisiana Fish fry
- 1 tablespoon olive oil
- 1 tablespoon parsley, chopped
- 1 lemon, sliced
- Fresh herbs, to garnish

Directions:
1. Mix fish fry with olive oil, and parsley then liberally rub over the catfish.
2. Place two fillets in each of the crisper plate.
3. Return the crisper plates to the Ninja Foodi Dual Zone Air Fryer.
4. Choose the Air Fry mode for Zone 1 and set the temperature to 390 degrees F and the time to 17 minutes|
5. Select the "MATCH" button to copy the settings for Zone 2.
6. Initiate cooking by pressing the START/STOP button.
7. Garnish with lemon slices and herbs.
8. Serve warm.

Salmon With Fennel Salad

Servings: 4
Cooking Time: 17 Minutes
Ingredients:
- 2 teaspoons fresh parsley, chopped
- 1 teaspoon fresh thyme, chopped
- 1 teaspoon salt
- 4 (6-oz) skinless center-cut salmon fillets
- 2 tablespoons olive oil
- 4 cups fennel, sliced
- ⅔ cup Greek yogurt
- 1 garlic clove, grated
- 2 tablespoons orange juice
- 1 teaspoon lemon juice
- 2 tablespoons fresh dill, chopped

Directions:
1. Preheat your Ninja Foodi Dual Zone Air Fryer to 200 degrees F.
2. Mix ½ teaspoon of salt, thyme, and parsley in a small bowl.
3. Brush the salmon with oil first, then rub liberally rub the herb mixture.
4. Place 2 salmon fillets in each of the crisper plate.
5. Return the crisper plate to the Ninja Foodi Dual Zone Air Fryer.
6. Choose the Air Fry mode for Zone 1 and set the temperature to 390 degrees F and the time to 17 minutes|
7. Select the "MATCH" button to copy the settings for Zone 2.
8. Initiate cooking by pressing the START/STOP button.
9. Meanwhile, mix fennel with garlic, yogurt, lemon juice, orange juice, remaining salt, and dill in a mixing bowl.
10. Serve the air fried salmon fillets with fennel salad.
11. Enjoy.

Chicken Thighs With Brussels Sprouts

Servings:2
Cooking Time:30
Ingredients:
- 2 tablespoons of honey
- 4 tablespoons of Dijon mustard
- Salt and black pepper, to tat
- 4 tablespoons of olive oil
- 1-1/2 cup Brussels sprouts
- 8 chicken thighs, skinless

Directions:
1. Take a bowl and add chicken thighs to it.
2. Add honey, Dijon mustard, salt, pepper, and 2 tablespoons of olive oil to the thighs.
3. Coat the chicken well and marinate it for 1 hour.
4. Now when start cooking season the Brussels sprouts with salt and black pepper along with remaining olive oil.
5. Put the chicken in the zone 1 basket.
6. Put the Brussels sprouts into the zone 2 basket.
7. Select ROAST function for chicken and set time to 30 minutes at 390 degrees F.
8. Select AIR FRY function for Brussels sprouts and set the timer to 20 at 400 degrees F.
9. Once done, serve and enjoy.

Nutrition:
- (Per serving) Calories1454 | Fat 72.2g| Sodium 869mg | Carbs 23g | Fiber 2.7g | Sugar 19g | Protein 172g

Sole And Cauliflower Fritters And Prawn Bake

Servings: 6
Cooking Time: 24 Minutes
Ingredients:
- Sole and Cauliflower Fritters:
- 230 g sole fillets
- 230 g mashed cauliflower
- 75 g red onion, chopped
- 1 bell pepper, finely chopped
- 1 egg, beaten
- 2 garlic cloves, minced
- 2 tablespoons fresh parsley, chopped
- 1 tablespoon olive oil
- 1 tablespoon coconut aminos or tamari
- ½ teaspoon scotch bonnet pepper, minced
- ½ teaspoon paprika
- Salt and white pepper, to taste
- Cooking spray
- Prawn Bake:
- 400 g prawns, peeled and deveined
- 1 egg, beaten
- 120 ml coconut milk
- 120 g Cheddar cheese, shredded
- ½ teaspoon coconut oil
- 1 teaspoon ground coriander

Directions:
1. Make the Sole and Cauliflower Fritters :
2. 1. Preheat the air fryer to 200°C. Spray the zone 1 air fryer basket with cooking spray. Place the sole fillets in the basket and air fry for 10 minutes, flipping them halfway through. 3. When the fillets are done, transfer them to a large bowl. Mash the fillets into flakes. Add the remaining ingredients and stir to combine. 4. Make the fritters: Scoop out 2 tablespoons of the fish mixture and shape into a patty about ½ inch thick with your hands. Repeat with the remaining fish mixture. 5. Arrange the patties in the zone 1 air fryer basket and bake for 14 minutes, flipping the patties halfway through, or until they are golden brown and cooked through. 6. Cool for 5 minutes and serve on a plate.
3. Make the Prawn Bake :
4. In the mixing bowl, mix prawns with egg, coconut milk, Cheddar cheese, coconut oil, and ground coriander.
5. Then put the mixture in the baking ramekins and put in the zone 2 air fryer basket.
6. Cook the prawns at 205°C for 5 minutes.

Glazed Scallops

Servings: 6
Cooking Time: 13 Minutes
Ingredients:
- 12 scallops
- 3 tablespoons olive oil
- Black pepper and salt to taste

Directions:
1. Rub the scallops with olive oil, black pepper, and salt.
2. Divide the scallops in the two crisper plates.
3. Return the crisper plate to the Ninja Foodi Dual Zone Air Fryer.
4. Choose the Air Fry mode for Zone 1 and set the temperature to 390 degrees F and the time to 13 minutes|
5. Select the "MATCH" button to copy the settings for Zone 2.
6. Initiate cooking by pressing the START/STOP button.
7. Flip the scallops once cooked halfway through, and resume cooking.
8. Serve warm.

Honey Teriyaki Tilapia

Servings: 4
Cooking Time: 10 Minutes
Ingredients:
- 8 tablespoons low-sodium teriyaki sauce
- 3 tablespoons honey
- 2 garlic cloves, minced
- 2 tablespoons extra virgin olive oil
- 3 pieces tilapia (each cut into 2 pieces)

Directions:
1. Combine all the first 4 ingredients to make the marinade.
2. Pour the marinade over the tilapia and let it sit for 20 minutes.
3. Place a crisper plate in each drawer. Place the tilapia in the drawers. Insert the drawers into the unit.
4. Select zone 1, then AIR FRY, then set the temperature to 360 degrees F/ 180 degrees C with a 10-minute timer. To match zone 2 settings to zone 1, choose MATCH. To begin, select START/STOP.
5. Remove the tilapia from the drawers after the timer has finished.

Nutrition:
- (Per serving) Calories 350 | Fat 16.4g | Sodium 706mg | Carbs 19.3g | Fiber 0.1g | Sugar 19g | Protein 29.3g

"fried" Fish With Seasoned Potato Wedges

Servings: 4
Cooking Time: 30 Minutes
Ingredients:
- FOR THE FISH
- 4 cod fillets (6 ounces each)
- 4 tablespoons all-purpose flour, divided
- ¼ cup cornstarch
- 1 teaspoon baking powder
- ¼ teaspoon kosher salt
- ⅓ cup lager-style beer or sparkling water
- Tartar sauce, cocktail sauce, or malt vinegar, for serving (optional)
- FOR THE POTATOES
- 4 russet potatoes
- 2 tablespoons vegetable oil
- ½ teaspoon paprika
- ½ teaspoon kosher salt
- ¼ teaspoon garlic powder
- ¼ teaspoon freshly ground black pepper

Directions:
1. To prep the fish: Pat the fish dry with a paper towel and coat lightly with 2 tablespoons of flour.
2. In a shallow dish, combine the remaining 2 tablespoons of flour, the cornstarch, baking powder, and salt. Stir in the beer to form a thick batter.
3. Dip the fish in the batter to coat both sides, then let rest on a cutting board for 10 minutes.
4. To prep the potatoes: Cut each potato in half lengthwise, then cut each half into 4 wedges.
5. In a large bowl, combine the potatoes and oil. Toss well to fully coat the potatoes. Add the paprika, salt, garlic powder, and black pepper and toss well to coat.
6. To cook the fish and potato wedges: Install a crisper plate in each of the two baskets. Place a piece of parchment paper or aluminum foil over the plate in the Zone 1 basket. Place the fish in the basket and insert the basket in the unit. Place the potato wedges in a single layer in the Zone 2 basket and insert the basket in the unit.
7. Select Zone 1, select AIR FRY, set the temperature to 400°F, and set the timer to 13 minutes.
8. Select Zone 2, select AIR FRY, set the temperature to 400°F, and set the timer to 30 minutes. Select SMART FINISH.
9. Press START/PAUSE to begin cooking.
10. When the Zone 1 timer reads 5 minutes, press START/PAUSE. Remove the basket and use a silicone spatula to carefully flip the fish over. Reinsert the basket and press START/PAUSE to resume cooking.
11. When cooking is complete, the fish should be cooked through and the potatoes crispy outside and tender inside. Serve hot with tartar sauce, cocktail sauce, or malt vinegar (if using).

Nutrition:
- (Per serving) Calories: 360; Total fat: 8g; Saturated fat: 1g; Carbohydrates: 40g; Fiber: 2g; Protein: 30g; Sodium: 302mg

Coconut Cream Mackerel

Servings: 4
Cooking Time: 6 Minutes
Ingredients:
- 900 g mackerel fillet
- 240 ml coconut cream
- 1 teaspoon ground coriander
- 1 teaspoon cumin seeds
- 1 garlic clove, peeled, chopped

Directions:
1. Chop the mackerel roughly and sprinkle it with coconut cream, ground coriander, cumin seeds, and garlic.
2. Then put the fish in the two air fryer drawers and cook at 204°C for 6 minutes.

Poultry Recipes

Asian Chicken Drumsticks

Servings: 4
Cooking Time: 20 Minutes
Ingredients:
- 8 chicken drumsticks
- 1 lime juice
- 30ml rice wine
- 45ml fish sauce
- 2 tbsp garlic, minced
- 55g brown sugar
- ½ tsp Sriracha sauce
- 1 tsp black pepper
- 1 tsp sesame oil
- Salt

Directions:
1. Add chicken drumsticks and remaining ingredients into the bowl and mix well. Cover and place in refrigerator for 4 hours.
2. Insert a crisper plate in the Ninja Foodi air fryer baskets.
3. Place the marinated chicken drumsticks in both baskets.
4. Select zone 1, then select "air fry" mode and set the temperature to 360 degrees F for 20 minutes. Press "match" to match zone 2 settings to zone 1. Press "start/stop" to begin.

Nutrition:
- (Per serving) Calories 225 | Fat 6.4g |Sodium 1223mg | Carbs 14.6g | Fiber 0.2g | Sugar 11.3g | Protein 26.3g

Ranch Turkey Tenders With Roasted Vegetable Salad

Servings: 4
Cooking Time: 20 Minutes
Ingredients:
- FOR THE TURKEY TENDERS
- 1 pound turkey tenderloin
- ¼ cup ranch dressing
- ½ cup panko bread crumbs
- Nonstick cooking spray
- FOR THE VEGETABLE SALAD
- 1 large sweet potato, peeled and diced
- 1 zucchini, diced
- 1 red bell pepper, diced
- 1 small red onion, sliced
- 1 tablespoon vegetable oil
- ¼ teaspoon kosher salt
- ½ teaspoon freshly ground black pepper
- 2 cups baby spinach
- ½ cup store-bought balsamic vinaigrette
- ¼ cup chopped walnuts

Directions:
1. To prep the turkey tenders: Slice the turkey crosswise into 16 strips. Brush both sides of each strip with ranch dressing, then coat with the panko. Press the bread crumbs into the turkey to help them adhere. Mist both sides of the strips with cooking spray.
2. To prep the vegetables: In a large bowl, combine the sweet potato, zucchini, bell pepper, onion, and vegetable oil. Stir well to coat the vegetables. Season with the salt and black pepper.
3. To cook the turkey and vegetables:
4. Install a crisper plate in the Zone 1 basket. Place the turkey tenders in the basket in a single layer and insert the basket in the unit. Place the vegetables in the Zone 2 basket and insert the basket in the unit.
5. Select Zone 1, select AIR FRY, set the temperature to 375°F, and set the time to 20 minutes.
6. Select Zone 2, select ROAST, set the temperature to 400°F, and set the time to 20 minutes. Select SMART FINISH.
7. Press START/PAUSE to begin cooking.
8. When both timers read 10 minutes, press START/PAUSE. Remove the Zone 1 basket and use silicone-tipped tongs to flip the turkey tenders. Reinsert the basket in the unit. Remove the Zone 2 basket and shake to redistribute the vegetables. Reinsert the basket and press START/PAUSE to resume cooking.
9. When cooking is complete, the turkey will be golden brown and cooked through and the vegetables will be fork-tender.
10. Place the spinach in a large serving bowl. Mix in the roasted vegetables and balsamic vinaigrette. Sprinkle with walnuts. Serve warm with the turkey tenders.

Thai Chicken With Cucumber And Chili Salad

Servings: 6
Cooking Time: 25 Minutes
Ingredients:
- 2 (570 g) small chickens, giblets discarded
- 1 tablespoon fish sauce
- 6 tablespoons chopped fresh coriander
- 2 teaspoons lime zest
- 1 teaspoon ground coriander
- 2 garlic cloves, minced
- 2 tablespoons packed light brown sugar
- 2 teaspoons vegetable oil
- Salt and ground black pepper, to taste
- 1 English cucumber, halved lengthwise and sliced thin
- 1 Thai chili, stemmed, deseeded, and minced
- 2 tablespoons chopped dry-roasted peanuts
- 1 small shallot, sliced thinly
- 1 tablespoon lime juice
- Lime wedges, for serving
- Cooking spray

Directions:
1. Arrange a chicken on a clean work surface, remove the backbone with kitchen shears, then pound the chicken breast to flat. Cut the breast in half. Repeat with the remaining chicken.
2. Loose the breast and thigh skin with your fingers, then pat the chickens dry and pierce about 10 holes into the fat deposits of the chickens. Tuck the wings under the chickens.
3. Combine 2 teaspoons of fish sauce, coriander, lime zest, coriander, garlic, 4 teaspoons of sugar, 1 teaspoon of vegetable oil, ½ teaspoon of salt, and ⅛ teaspoon of ground black pepper in a small bowl. Stir to mix well.
4. Rub the fish sauce mixture under the breast and thigh skin of the game chickens, then let sit for 10 minutes to marinate.
5. Preheat the air fryer to 200ºC. Spritz the two air fryer baskets with cooking spray.
6. Arrange the marinated chickens in the preheated air fryer, skin side down.
7. Air fry for 15 minutes, then gently turn the game hens over and air fry for 10 more minutes or until the skin is golden brown and the internal temperature of the chickens reads at least 75ºC.
8. Meanwhile, combine all the remaining ingredients, except for the lime wedges, in a large bowl and sprinkle with salt and black pepper. Toss to mix well.
9. Transfer the fried chickens on a large plate, then sit the salad aside and squeeze the lime wedges over before serving.

Chicken And Potatoes

Servings: 2
Cooking Time: 10 Minutes
Ingredients:
- 2 potatoes, diced
- 2 chicken breasts, diced
- 4 cloves garlic crushed
- 2 teaspoons smoked paprika
- ½ teaspoon red chili flakes
- 1 teaspoon fresh thyme
- 1 teaspoon salt
- ¼ teaspoon black pepper
- 2 tablespoons olive oil

Directions:
1. Rub chicken with half of the salt, black pepper, oil, thyme, red chili flakes, paprika and garlic.
2. Mix potatoes with remaining spices, oil and garlic in a bowl.
3. Add chicken to one air fryer basket and potatoes the second basket.
4. Return the air fryer basket 1 to Zone 1, and basket 2 to Zone 2 of the Ninja Foodi 2-Basket Air Fryer.
5. Choose the "Air Fry" mode for Zone 1 at 375 degrees F and 10 minutes of cooking time.
6. Select the "MATCH COOK" option to copy the settings for Zone 2.
7. Initiate cooking by pressing the START/PAUSE BUTTON.
8. Flip the chicken and toss potatoes once cooked halfway through.
9. Garnish with chopped parsley.
10. Serve chicken with the potatoes.

Nutrition:
- (Per serving) Calories 374 | Fat 13g |Sodium 552mg | Carbs 25g | Fiber 1.2g | Sugar 1.2g | Protein 37.7g

Nashville Hot Chicken

Servings: 8
Cooking Time: 24 To 28 Minutes
Ingredients:
- 1.4 kg bone-in, skin-on chicken pieces, breasts halved crosswise
- 1 tablespoon sea salt
- 1 tablespoon freshly ground black pepper
- 140 g finely ground blanched almond flour
- 130 g grated Parmesan cheese
- 1 tablespoon baking powder
- 2 teaspoons garlic powder, divided
- 120 g heavy (whipping) cream
- 2 large eggs, beaten
- 1 tablespoon vinegar-based hot sauce
- Avocado oil spray
- 115 g unsalted butter
- 120 ml avocado oil
- 1 tablespoon cayenne pepper (more or less to taste)
- 2 tablespoons Xylitol

Directions:
1. Sprinkle the chicken with the salt and pepper.
2. In a large shallow bowl, whisk together the almond flour, Parmesan cheese, baking powder, and 1 teaspoon of the garlic powder.
3. In a separate bowl, whisk together the heavy cream, eggs, and hot sauce.
4. Dip the chicken pieces in the egg, then coat each with the almond flour mixture, pressing the mixture into the chicken to adhere. Allow to sit for 15 minutes to let the breading set.
5. Set the air fryer to 200°C. Place the chicken in a single layer in the two air fryer baskets, being careful not to overcrowd the pieces. Spray the chicken with oil and roast for 13 minutes.
6. Carefully flip the chicken and spray it with more oil. Reduce the air fryer temperature to 180°C. Roast for another 11 to 15 minutes, until an instant-read thermometer reads 70°C.
7. While the chicken cooks, heat the butter, avocado oil, cayenne pepper, xylitol, and remaining 1 teaspoon of garlic powder in a saucepan over medium-low heat. Cook until the butter is melted and the sugar substitute has dissolved.
8. Remove the chicken from the air fryer. Use tongs to dip the chicken in the sauce. Place the coated chicken on a rack over a baking sheet, and allow it to rest for 5 minutes before serving.

Crumbed Chicken Katsu

Servings: 4
Cooking Time: 26 Minutes
Ingredients:
- 1 lb. boneless chicken breast, cut in half
- 2 large eggs, beaten
- 1 ½ cups panko bread crumbs
- Salt and black pepper ground to taste
- Cooking spray
- Sauce:
- 1 tablespoon sugar
- 2 tablespoons soy sauce
- 1 tablespoon sherry
- ½ cup ketchup
- 2 teaspoons Worcestershire sauce
- 1 teaspoon garlic, minced

Directions:
1. Mix soy sauce, ketchup, sherry, sugar, garlic, and Worcestershire sauce in a mixing bowl.
2. Keep this katsu aside for a while.
3. Rub the chicken pieces with salt and black pepper.
4. Whisk eggs in a shallow dish and spread breadcrumbs in another tray.
5. Dip the chicken in the egg mixture and coat them with breadcrumbs.
6. Place the coated chicken in the two crisper plates and spray them with cooking spray.
7. Return the crisper plate to the Ninja Foodi Dual Zone Air Fryer.
8. Choose the Air Fry mode for Zone 1 and set the temperature to 390 degrees F and the time to 26 minutes|
9. Select the "MATCH" button to copy the settings for Zone 2.
10. Initiate cooking by pressing the START/STOP button.
11. Flip the chicken once cooked halfway through, then resume cooking.
12. Serve warm with the sauce.

Almond Chicken

Servings: 4
Cooking Time: 25 Minutes
Ingredients:
- 2 large eggs
- ½ cup buttermilk
- 2 teaspoons garlic salt
- 1 teaspoon pepper
- 2 cups slivered almonds, finely chopped
- 4 boneless, skinless chicken breast halves (6 ounces each)

Directions:
1. Whisk together the egg, buttermilk, garlic salt, and pepper in a small bowl.
2. In another small bowl, place the almonds.
3. Dip the chicken in the egg mixture, then roll it in the almonds, patting it down to help the coating stick.
4. Install a crisper plate in both drawers. Place half the chicken breasts in the zone 1 drawer and half in zone 2's, then insert the drawers into the unit.
5. Select zone 1, select AIR FRY, set temperature to 390 degrees F/ 200 degrees C, and set time to 22 minutes. Select MATCH to match zone 2 settings to zone 1. Press the START/STOP button to begin cooking.
6. When the time reaches 11 minutes, press START/STOP to pause the unit. Remove the drawers and flip the chicken. Re-insert the drawers into the unit and press START/STOP to resume cooking.
7. When cooking is complete, remove the chicken.

Nutrition:
- (Per serving) Calories 353 | Fat 18g | Sodium 230mg | Carbs 6g | Fiber 2g | Sugar 3g | Protein 41g

Cheddar-stuffed Chicken

Servings: 4
Cooking Time: 20 Minutes
Ingredients:
- 3 bacon strips, cooked and crumbled
- 2 ounces Cheddar cheese, cubed
- ¼ cup barbeque sauce
- 2 (4 ounces) boneless chicken breasts
- Salt and black pepper to taste

Directions:
1. Make a 1-inch deep pouch in each chicken breast.
2. Mix cheddar cubes with half of the BBQ sauce, salt, black pepper, and bacon.
3. Divide this filling in the chicken breasts and secure the edges with a toothpick.
4. Brush the remaining BBQ sauce over the chicken breasts.
5. Place the chicken in the crisper plate and spray them with cooking oil.
6. Return the crisper plate to the Ninja Foodi Dual Zone Air Fryer.
7. Choose the Air Fry mode for Zone 1 and set the temperature to 360 degrees F and the time to 20 minutes|
8. Initiate cooking by pressing the START/STOP button.
9. Serve warm.

Wild Rice And Kale Stuffed Chicken Thighs

Servings: 4
Cooking Time: 22 Minutes
Ingredients:
- 4 boneless, skinless chicken thighs
- 250 g cooked wild rice
- 35 g chopped kale
- 2 garlic cloves, minced
- 1 teaspoon salt
- Juice of 1 lemon
- 100 g crumbled feta
- Olive oil cooking spray
- 1 tablespoon olive oi

Directions:
1. Preheat the air fryer to 192°C.
2. Place the chicken thighs between two pieces of plastic wrap, and using a meat mallet or a rolling pin, pound them out to about ¼-inch thick.
3. In a medium bowl, combine the rice, kale, garlic, salt, and lemon juice and mix well.
4. Place a quarter of the rice mixture into the middle of each chicken thigh, then sprinkle 2 tablespoons of feta over the filling.
5. Spray the two air fryer drawers with olive oil cooking spray.
6. Fold the sides of the chicken thigh over the filling, and then gently place each of them seam-side down into the two air fryer drawers. Brush each stuffed chicken thigh with olive oil.
7. Roast the stuffed chicken thighs for 12 minutes, then turn them over and cook for an additional 10 minutes, or until the internal temperature reaches 76°C.

Sweet-and-sour Chicken With Pineapple Cauliflower Rice

Servings: 4
Cooking Time: 30 Minutes

Ingredients:
- FOR THE CHICKEN
- ¼ cup cornstarch, plus 2 teaspoons
- ¼ teaspoon kosher salt
- 2 large eggs
- 1 tablespoon sesame oil
- 1½ pounds boneless, skinless chicken breasts, cut into 1-inch pieces
- Nonstick cooking spray
- 6 tablespoons ketchup
- ¾ cup apple cider vinegar
- 1½ tablespoons soy sauce
- 1 tablespoon sugar
- FOR THE CAULIFLOWER RICE
- 1 cup finely diced fresh pineapple
- 1 red bell pepper, thinly sliced
- 1 small red onion, thinly sliced
- 1 tablespoon vegetable oil
- 2 cups frozen cauliflower rice, thawed
- 2 tablespoons soy sauce
- 1 teaspoon sesame oil
- 2 scallions, sliced

Directions:
1. To prep the chicken:
2. Set up a breading station with two small shallow bowls. Combine ¼ cup of cornstarch and the salt in the first bowl. In the second bowl, beat the eggs with the sesame oil.
3. Dip the chicken pieces in the cornstarch mixture to coat, then into the egg mixture, then back into the cornstarch mixture to coat. Mist the coated pieces with cooking spray.
4. In a small bowl, whisk together the ketchup, vinegar, soy sauce, sugar, and remaining 2 teaspoons of cornstarch.
5. To prep the cauliflower rice: Blot the pineapple dry with a paper towel. In a large bowl, combine the pineapple, bell pepper, onion, and vegetable oil.
6. To cook the chicken and cauliflower rice: Install a crisper plate in each of the two baskets. Place the chicken in the Zone 1 basket and insert the basket in the unit. Place a piece of aluminum foil over the crisper plate in the Zone 2 basket and add the pineapple mixture. Insert the basket in the unit.
7. Select Zone 1, select AIR FRY, set the temperature to 400°F, and set the time to 30 minutes.
8. Select Zone 2, select AIR BROIL, set the temperature to 450°F, and set the time to 12 minutes. Select SMART FINISH.
9. Press START/PAUSE to begin cooking.
10. When the Zone 2 timer reads 4 minutes, press START/PAUSE. Remove the basket and stir in the cauliflower rice, soy sauce, and sesame oil. Reinsert the basket and press START/PAUSE to resume cooking.
11. When cooking is complete, the chicken will be golden brown and cooked through and the rice warmed through. Stir the scallions into the rice and serve.

Wings With Corn On The Cob

Servings: 2
Cooking Time: 40 Minutes

Ingredients:
- 6 chicken wings, skinless
- 2 tablespoons coconut amino
- 2 tablespoons brown sugar
- 1 teaspoon ginger, paste
- ½ inch garlic, minced
- Salt and black pepper to taste
- 2 corn on cobs, small
- Oil spray, for greasing

Directions:
1. Spray the corns with oil spray and season them with salt.
2. Coat the chicken wings with coconut amino, brown sugar, ginger, garlic, salt, and black pepper.
3. Spray the wings with a good amount of oil spray.
4. Put the chicken wings in the zone 1 basket.
5. Put the corn into the zone 2 basket.
6. Select ROAST mode for the chicken wings and set the time to 23 minutes at 400 degrees F/ 200 degrees C.
7. Press 2 and select the AIR FRY mode for the corn and set the time to 40 at 300 degrees F/ 150 degrees C.
8. Once it's done, serve and enjoy.

Nutrition:
- (Per serving) Calories 950 | Fat 33.4g | Sodium 592 mg | Carbs 27.4g | Fiber 2.1g | Sugar 11.3 g | Protein 129g

Chicken Thighs In Waffles

Servings: 4
Cooking Time: 40 Minutes
Ingredients:
- For the chicken:
- 4 chicken thighs, skin on
- 240 ml low-fat buttermilk
- 65 g all-purpose flour
- ½ teaspoon garlic powder
- ½ teaspoon mustard powder
- 1 teaspoon kosher salt
- ½ teaspoon freshly ground black pepper
- 85 g honey, for serving
- Cooking spray
- For the waffles:
- 65 g all-purpose flour
- 65 g whole wheat pastry flour
- 1 large egg, beaten
- 240 ml low-fat buttermilk
- 1 teaspoon baking powder
- 2 tablespoons rapeseed oil
- ½ teaspoon kosher salt
- 1 tablespoon granulated sugar

Directions:
1. Combine the chicken thighs with buttermilk in a large bowl. Wrap the bowl in plastic and refrigerate to marinate for at least an hour. 2. Preheat the air fryer to 180°C. Spritz the two air fryer baskets with cooking spray. 3. Combine the flour, mustard powder, garlic powder, salt, and black pepper in a shallow dish. Stir to mix well. 4. Remove the thighs from the buttermilk and pat dry with paper towels. Sit the bowl of buttermilk aside. 5. Dip the thighs in the flour mixture first, then into the buttermilk, and then into the flour mixture. Shake the excess off. 6. Arrange the thighs in the two preheated air fryer baskets and spritz with cooking spray. Air fryer for 20 minutes or until an instant-read thermometer inserted in the thickest part of the chicken thighs registers at least 75°C. Flip the thighs halfway through. 7. Meanwhile, make the waffles: combine the ingredients for the waffles in a large bowl. Stir to mix well, then arrange the mixture in a waffle iron and cook until a golden and fragrant waffle forms. 8. Remove the waffles from the waffle iron and slice into 4 pieces. Remove the chicken thighs from the air fryer and allow to cool for 5 minutes. 9. Arrange each chicken thigh on each waffle piece and drizzle with 1 tablespoon of honey. Serve warm.

Lemon-pepper Chicken Thighs With Buttery Roasted Radishes

Servings: 4
Cooking Time: 28 Minutes
Ingredients:
- FOR THE CHICKEN
- 4 bone-in, skin-on chicken thighs (6 ounces each)
- 1 teaspoon olive oil
- 2 teaspoons lemon pepper
- ¼ teaspoon kosher salt
- FOR THE RADISHES
- 1 bunch radishes (greens removed), halved through the stem
- 1 teaspoon olive oil
- ¼ teaspoon kosher salt
- ¼ teaspoon freshly ground black pepper
- 1 tablespoon unsalted butter, cut into small pieces
- 2 tablespoons chopped fresh parsley

Directions:
1. To prep the chicken: Brush both sides of the chicken thighs with olive oil, then season with lemon pepper and salt.
2. To prep the radishes: In a large bowl, combine the radishes, olive oil, salt, and black pepper. Stir well to coat the radishes.
3. To cook the chicken and radishes: Install a crisper plate in each of the two baskets. Place the chicken skin-side up in the Zone 1 basket and insert the basket in the unit. Place the radishes in the Zone 2 basket and insert the basket in the unit.
4. Select Zone 1, select AIR FRY, set the temperature to 390°F, and set the time to 28 minutes.
5. Select Zone 2, select ROAST, set the temperature to 400°F, and set the time to 15 minutes. Select SMART FINISH.
6. Press START/PAUSE to begin cooking.
7. When the Zone 2 timer reads 5 minutes, press START/PAUSE. Remove the basket, scatter the butter pieces over the radishes, and reinsert the basket. Press START/PAUSE to resume cooking.
8. When cooking is complete, the chicken should be cooked through and the radishes will be soft. Stir the parsley into the radishes and serve.

Roasted Garlic Chicken Pizza With Cauliflower "wings"

Servings: 4
Cooking Time: 25 Minutes
Ingredients:
- FOR THE PIZZA
- 2 prebaked rectangular pizza crusts or flatbreads
- 2 tablespoons olive oil
- 1 tablespoon minced garlic
- 1½ cups shredded part-skim mozzarella cheese
- 6 ounces boneless, skinless chicken breast, thinly sliced
- ¼ teaspoon red pepper flakes (optional)
- FOR THE CAULIFLOWER "WINGS"
- 4 cups cauliflower florets
- 1 tablespoon vegetable oil
- ½ cup Buffalo wing sauce

Directions:
1. To prep the pizza:
2. Trim the pizza crusts to fit in the air fryer basket, if necessary.
3. Brush the top of each crust with the oil and sprinkle with the garlic. Top the crusts with the mozzarella, chicken, and red pepper flakes.
4. To prep the cauliflower "wings": In a large bowl, combine the cauliflower and oil and toss to coat the florets.
5. To cook the pizza and "wings":
6. Install a crisper plate in each of the two baskets. Place one pizza in the Zone 1 basket and insert the basket in the unit. Place the cauliflower in the Zone 2 basket and insert the basket in the unit.
7. Select Zone 1, select ROAST, set the temperature to 375°F, and set the time to 25 minutes.
8. Select Zone 2, select AIR FRY, set the temperature to 390°F, and set the time to 25 minutes. Select SMART FINISH.
9. Press START/PAUSE to begin cooking.
10. When the Zone 1 timer reads 13 minutes, press START/PAUSE. Remove the basket. Transfer the pizza to a cutting board. Add the second pizza to the basket. Reinsert the basket in the unit and press START/PAUSE to resume cooking.
11. When the Zone 2 timer reads 5 minutes, press START/PAUSE. Remove the basket and add the Buffalo wing sauce to the cauliflower. Shake well to evenly coat the cauliflower in the sauce. Reinsert the basket and press START/PAUSE to resume cooking.
12. When cooking is complete, the cauliflower will be crisp on the outside and tender inside, and the chicken on the second pizza will be cooked through and the cheese melted.
13. Cut each pizza into 4 slices. Serve with the cauliflower "wings" on the side.

Harissa-rubbed Chicken

Servings: 4
Cooking Time: 21 Minutes
Ingredients:
- Harissa:
- 120 ml olive oil
- 6 cloves garlic, minced
- 2 tablespoons smoked paprika
- 1 tablespoon ground coriander
- 1 tablespoon ground cumin
- 1 teaspoon ground caraway
- 1 teaspoon kosher salt
- ½ to 1 teaspoon cayenne pepper
- Chickens:
- 120 g yogurt
- 2 small chickens, any giblets removed, split in half lengthwise

Directions:
1. For the harissa: In a medium microwave-safe bowl, combine the oil, garlic, paprika, coriander, cumin, caraway, salt, and cayenne. Microwave on high for 1 minute, stirring halfway through the cooking time. 2. For the chicken: In a small bowl, combine 1 to 2 tablespoons harissa and the yogurt. Whisk until well combined. Place the chicken halves in a resealable plastic bag and pour the marinade over. Seal the bag and massage until all of the pieces are thoroughly coated. Marinate at room temperature for 30 minutes or in the refrigerator for up to 24 hours. 3. Arrange the hen halves in a single layer in the two air fryer drawers. Set the air fryer to 200°C for 20 minutes. Use a meat thermometer to ensure the chickens have reached an internal temperature of 76°C.

Balsamic Duck Breast

Servings: 2
Cooking Time: 20 Minutes
Ingredients:
- 2 duck breasts
- 1 teaspoon parsley
- Salt and black pepper, to taste
- Marinade:
- 1 tablespoon olive oil
- ½ teaspoon French mustard
- 1 teaspoon dried garlic
- 2 teaspoons honey
- ½ teaspoon balsamic vinegar

Directions:
1. Mix olive oil, mustard, garlic, honey, and balsamic vinegar in a bowl.
2. Add duck breasts to the marinade and rub well.
3. Place one duck breast in each crisper plate.
4. Return the crisper plates to the Ninja Foodi Dual Zone Air Fryer.
5. Choose the Air Fry mode for Zone 1 and set the temperature to 360 degrees F and the time to 20 minutes|
6. Select the "MATCH" button to copy the settings for Zone 2.
7. Initiate cooking by pressing the START/STOP button.
8. Flip the duck breasts once cooked halfway through, then resume cooking.
9. Serve warm.

Garlic Parmesan Drumsticks

Servings: 4
Cooking Time: 25 Minutes
Ingredients:
- 8 (115 g) chicken drumsticks
- ½ teaspoon salt
- ⅛ teaspoon ground black pepper
- ½ teaspoon garlic powder
- 2 tablespoons salted butter, melted
- 45 g grated Parmesan cheese
- 1 tablespoon dried parsley

Directions:
1. Sprinkle drumsticks with salt, pepper, and garlic powder. Place drumsticks into the two ungreased air fryer baskets.
2. Adjust the temperature to 200°C and air fry for 25 minutes, turning drumsticks halfway through cooking. Drumsticks will be golden and have an internal temperature of at least 75°C when done.
3. Transfer drumsticks to a large serving dish. Pour butter over drumsticks, and sprinkle with Parmesan and parsley. Serve warm.

Brazilian Chicken Drumsticks

Servings: 6
Cooking Time: 47 Minutes
Ingredients:
- 2 teaspoons cumin seeds
- 2 teaspoons dried parsley
- 2 teaspoons turmeric powder
- 2 teaspoons dried oregano leaves
- 2 teaspoons salt
- 1 teaspoon coriander seeds
- 1 teaspoon black peppercorns
- 1 teaspoon cayenne pepper
- ½ cup lime juice
- 4 tablespoons vegetable oil
- 3 lbs. chicken drumsticks

Directions:
1. Grind cumin, parsley, salt, coriander seeds, cayenne pepper, peppercorns, oregano, and turmeric in a food processor.
2. Add this mixture to lemon juice and oil in a bowl and mix well.
3. Rub the spice paste over the chicken drumsticks and let them marinate for 30 minutes|
4. Divide the chicken drumsticks in both the crisper plates.
5. Return the crisper plates to the Ninja Foodi Dual Zone Air Fryer.
6. Choose the Air Fry mode for Zone 1 and set the temperature to 390 degrees F and the time to 47 minutes|
7. Select the "MATCH" button to copy the settings for Zone 2.
8. Initiate cooking by pressing the START/STOP button.
9. Flip the drumsticks when cooked halfway through, then resume cooking.
10. Serve warm.

Thai Curry Meatballs

Servings: 4
Cooking Time: 10 Minutes
Ingredients:
- 450 g chicken mince
- 15 g chopped fresh coriander
- 1 teaspoon chopped fresh mint
- 1 tablespoon fresh lime juice
- 1 tablespoon Thai red, green, or yellow curry paste
- 1 tablespoon fish sauce
- 2 garlic cloves, minced
- 2 teaspoons minced fresh ginger
- ½ teaspoon kosher salt
- ½ teaspoon black pepper
- ¼ teaspoon red pepper flakes

Directions:
1. Preheat the zone 1 air fryer drawer to 200°C.
2. In a large bowl, gently mix the chicken mince, coriander, mint, lime juice, curry paste, fish sauce, garlic, ginger, salt, black pepper, and red pepper flakes until thoroughly combined.
3. Form the mixture into 16 meatballs. Place the meatballs in a single layer in the zone 1 air fryer drawer. Air fry for 10 minutes, turning the meatballs halfway through the cooking time. Use a meat thermometer to ensure the meatballs have reached an internal temperature of 76°C. Serve immediately.

Easy Chicken Thighs

Servings: 8
Cooking Time: 12 Minutes
Ingredients:
- 900g chicken thighs, boneless & skinless
- 2 tsp chilli powder
- 2 tsp olive oil
- 1 tsp garlic powder
- 1 tsp ground cumin
- Pepper
- Salt

Directions:
1. In a bowl, mix chicken with remaining ingredients until well coated.
2. Insert a crisper plate in the Ninja Foodi air fryer baskets.
3. Place chicken thighs in both baskets.
4. Select zone 1 then select "air fry" mode and set the temperature to 390 degrees F for 12 minutes. Press "match" to match zone 2 settings to zone 1. Press "start/stop" to begin. Turn halfway through.

Nutrition:
- (Per serving) Calories 230 | Fat 9.7g | Sodium 124mg | Carbs 0.7g | Fiber 0.3g | Sugar 0.2g | Protein 33g

Bacon Wrapped Stuffed Chicken

Servings: 4
Cooking Time: 25 Minutes
Ingredients:
- 3 boneless chicken breasts
- 6 jalapenos, sliced
- ¾ cup (170g) cream cheese
- ½ cup Monterey Jack cheese, shredded
- 1 teaspoon ground cumin
- 12 strips thick bacon

Directions:
1. Cut the chicken breasts in half crosswise and pound them with a mallet.
2. Mix cream cheese with cumin and Monterey jacket cheese in a bowl.
3. Spread the cream cheese mixture over the chicken breast slices.
4. Add jalapeno slices on top and wrap the chicken slices.
5. Wrap each chicken rolls with a bacon slice.
6. Place the wrapped rolls into the Ninja Foodi 2 Baskets Air Fryer baskets.
7. Return the air fryer basket 1 to Zone 1, and basket 2 to Zone 2 of the Ninja Foodi 2-Basket Air Fryer.
8. Choose the "Air Fry" mode for Zone 1 at 340 degrees F and 25 minutes of cooking time.
9. Select the "MATCH COOK" option to copy the settings for Zone 2.
10. Initiate cooking by pressing the START/PAUSE BUTTON.
11. Serve warm.

Nutrition:
- (Per serving) Calories 220 | Fat 1.7g | Sodium 178mg | Carbs 1.7g | Fiber 0.2g | Sugar 0.2g | Protein 32.9g

Crispy Dill Chicken Strips

Servings: 4
Cooking Time: 10 Minutes
Ingredients:
- 2 whole boneless, skinless chicken breasts (about 450 g each), halved lengthwise
- 230 ml Italian dressing
- 110 g finely crushed crisps
- 1 tablespoon dried dill weed
- 1 tablespoon garlic powder
- 1 large egg, beaten
- 1 to 2 tablespoons oil

Directions:
1. In a large resealable bag, combine the chicken and Italian dressing. Seal the bag and refrigerate to marinate at least 1 hour.
2. In a shallow dish, stir together the potato chips, dill, and garlic powder. Place the beaten egg in a second shallow dish.
3. Remove the chicken from the marinade. Roll the chicken pieces in the egg and the crisp mixture, coating thoroughly.
4. Preheat the air fryer to 170°C. Line the two air fryer drawers with parchment paper.
5. Place the coated chicken on the parchment and spritz with oil.
6. Cook for 5 minutes. Flip the chicken, spritz it with oil, and cook for 5 minutes more until the outsides are crispy and the insides are no longer pink.

Chicken Drumsticks

Servings: 6
Cooking Time: 15 Minutes
Ingredients:
- 12 chicken drumsticks
- 72g chilli garlic sauce
- 2 tbsp ginger, minced
- 1 tbsp garlic, minced
- 3 green onion stalks, chopped
- 60ml orange juice
- 60ml soy sauce
- ½ medium onion, sliced
- Pepper
- Salt

Directions:
1. Add all the ingredients except the drumsticks into a blender and blend until smooth.
2. Place the chicken drumsticks in bowl.
3. Pour the blended mixture over chicken drumsticks and mix well.
4. Cover the bowl and place in refrigerator for 1 hour.
5. Insert a crisper plate in the Ninja Foodi air fryer baskets.
6. Place the marinated chicken drumsticks in both baskets.
7. Select zone 1 then select "air fry" mode and set the temperature to 390 degrees F for 15 minutes. Press "match" and then "start/stop" to begin.

Nutrition:
- (Per serving) Calories 178 | Fat 5.4g | Sodium 701mg | Carbs 4.5g | Fiber 0.6g | Sugar 1.5g | Protein 26.4g

Chicken Leg Piece

Servings: 1
Cooking Time: 25
Ingredients:
- 1 teaspoon of onion powder
- 1 teaspoon of paprika powder
- 1 teaspoon of garlic powder
- Salt and black pepper, to taste
- 1 tablespoon of Italian seasoning
- 1 teaspoon of celery seeds
- 2 eggs, whisked
- 1/3 cup buttermilk
- 1 cup of corn flour
- 1 pound of chicken leg

Directions:
1. Take a bowl and whisk egg along with pepper, salt, and buttermilk.
2. Set it aside for further use.
3. Mix all the spices in a small separate bowl.
4. Dredge the chicken in egg wash then dredge it in seasoning.
5. Coat the chicken legs with oil spray.
6. At the end dust it with the corn flour.
7. Divide the leg pieces into two zones.
8. Set zone 1 basket to 400 degrees F, for 25 minutes.
9. Select MATCH for zone 2 basket.
10. Let the air fryer do the magic.
11. Once it's done, serve and enjoy.

Nutrition:
- (Per serving) Calories 1511| Fat 52.3g| Sodium 615 mg | Carbs 100g | Fiber 9.2g | Sugar 8.1g | Protein 154.2g

Chicken & Veggies

Servings: 4
Cooking Time: 10 Minutes
Ingredients:
- 450g chicken breast, boneless & cut into pieces
- 2 garlic cloves, minced
- 15ml olive oil
- 239g frozen mix vegetables
- 1 tbsp Italian seasoning
- ½ tsp chilli powder
- ½ tsp garlic powder
- Pepper
- Salt

Directions:
1. In a bowl, toss chicken with remaining ingredients until well coated.
2. Insert a crisper plate in the Ninja Foodi air fryer baskets.
3. Add chicken and vegetables in both baskets.
4. Select zone 1 then select "air fry" mode and set the temperature to 390 degrees F for 10 minutes. Press "match" to match zone 2 settings to zone 1. Press "start/stop" to begin.

Nutrition:
- (Per serving) Calories 221 | Fat 7.6g |Sodium 126mg | Carbs 10.6g | Fiber 3.3g | Sugar 2.7g | Protein 26.3g

Chicken Wings

Servings:3
Cooking Time:20
Ingredients:
- 1 cup chicken batter mix, Louisiana
- 9 Chicken wings
- ½ teaspoon of smoked paprika
- 2 tablespoons of Dijon mustard
- 1 tablespoon of cayenne pepper
- 1 teaspoon of meat tenderizer, powder
- oil spray, for greasing

Directions:
1. Pat dry chicken wings and add mustard, paprika, meat tenderizer, and cayenne pepper.
2. Dredge it in the chicken batter mix.
3. Oil sprays the chicken wings.
4. Grease both baskets of the air fryer.
5. Divide the wings between the two zones of the air fryer.
6. Set zone 1 to AR FRY mode at 400 degrees F for 20 minutes
7. Select MATCH for zone 2.
8. Hit start to begin with the cooking.
9. Once the cooking cycle complete, serve, and enjoy hot.

Nutrition:
- (Per serving) Calories621 | Fat 32.6g| Sodium 2016mg | Carbs 46.6g | Fiber 1.1g | Sugar 0.2g | Protein 32.1g

Sweet And Spicy Carrots With Chicken Thighs

Servings:2
Cooking Time:35
Ingredients:
- Cooking spray, for greasing
- 2 tablespoons butter, melted
- 1 tablespoon hot honey
- 1 teaspoon orange zest
- 1 teaspoon cardamom
- ½ pound baby carrots
- 1 tablespoon orange juice
- Salt and black pepper, to taste
- ½ pound of carrots, baby carrots
- 8 chicken thighs

Directions:
1. Take a bowl and mix all the glaze ingredients in it.
2. Now, coat the chicken and carrots with the glaze and let it rest for 30 minutes.
3. Now place the chicken thighs into the zone 1 basket.
4. Next put the glazed carrots into the zone 2 basket.
5. Press button 1 for the first basket and set it to ROAST Mode at 350 degrees F for 35 minutes.
6. For the second basket hit 2 and set time to AIRFRY mode at 390 degrees F for 8-10 minutes.
7. Once the cooking cycle completes take out the carrots and chicken and serve it hot.

Nutrition:
- (Per serving) Calories 1312| Fat 55.4g| Sodium 757mg | Carbs 23.3g | Fiber6.7 g | Sugar12 g | Protein171 g

Easy Cajun Chicken Drumsticks

Servings: 5
Cooking Time: 40 Minutes
Ingredients:
- 1 tablespoon olive oil
- 10 chicken drumsticks
- 1½ tablespoons Cajun seasoning
- Salt and ground black pepper, to taste

Directions:
1. Preheat the air fryer to 200°C. Grease the two air fryer drawers with olive oil. 2. On a clean work surface, rub the chicken drumsticks with Cajun seasoning, salt, and ground black pepper. 3. Arrange the seasoned chicken drumsticks in a single layer in the air fryer. 4. Air fry for 18 minutes or until lightly browned. Flip the drumsticks halfway through. 5. Remove the chicken drumsticks from the air fryer. Serve immediately.

Italian Chicken & Potatoes

Servings: 4
Cooking Time: 24 Minutes
Ingredients:
- 450g chicken breast, boneless & diced
- 30ml olive oil
- ½ tsp lemon zest
- 2 tbsp fresh lemon juice
- 450g baby potatoes, quartered
- 1 tbsp Greek seasoning
- Pepper
- Salt

Directions:
1. Toss potatoes with ½ tablespoon Greek seasoning, 1 tablespoon oil, lemon zest, lemon juice, pepper, and salt in a bowl.
2. Insert a crisper plate in the Ninja Foodi air fryer baskets.
3. Add potatoes into the zone 1 basket.
4. In a bowl, toss chicken with the remaining oil and seasoning.
5. Add the chicken into the zone 2 basket.
6. Select zone 1, then select "air fry" mode and set the temperature to 390 degrees F for 12 minutes. Press "match" to match zone 2 settings to zone 1. Press "start/stop" to begin.

Nutrition:
- (Per serving) Calories 262 | Fat 10.1g |Sodium 227mg | Carbs 15.5g | Fiber 2.9g | Sugar 0.2g | Protein 27.2g

African Piri-piri Chicken Drumsticks

Servings: 2
Cooking Time: 20 Minutes
Ingredients:
- Chicken:
- 1 tablespoon chopped fresh thyme leaves
- 1 tablespoon minced fresh ginger
- 1 small shallot, finely chopped
- 2 garlic cloves, minced
- 80 ml piri-piri sauce or hot sauce
- 3 tablespoons extra-virgin olive oil
- Zest and juice of 1 lemon
- 1 teaspoon smoked paprika
- ½ teaspoon kosher salt
- ½ teaspoon black pepper
- 4 chicken drumsticks
- Glaze:
- 2 tablespoons butter or ghee
- 1 teaspoon chopped fresh thyme leaves
- 1 garlic clove, minced
- 1 tablespoon piri-piri sauce
- 1 tablespoon fresh lemon juice

Directions:
1. For the chicken: In a small bowl, stir together all the ingredients except the chicken. Place the chicken and the marinade in a gallon-size resealable plastic bag. Seal the bag and massage to coat. Refrigerate for at least 2 hours or up to 24 hours, turning the bag occasionally. 2. Place the chicken legs in the zone 1 air fryer basket. Set the air fryer to 200°C for 20 minutes, turning the chicken halfway through the cooking time. 3. Meanwhile, for the glaze: Melt the butter in a small saucepan over medium-high heat. Add the thyme and garlic. Cook, stirring, until the garlic just begins to brown, 1 to 2 minutes. Add the piri-piri sauce and lemon juice. Reduce the heat to medium-low and simmer for 1 to 2 minutes. 4. Transfer the chicken to a serving platter. Pour the glaze over the chicken. Serve immediately.

Bell Pepper Stuffed Chicken Roll-ups

Servings: 4
Cooking Time: 12 Minutes

Ingredients:
- 2 (115 g) boneless, skinless chicken breasts, slice in half horizontally
- 1 tablespoon olive oil
- Juice of ½ lime
- 2 tablespoons taco seasoning
- ½ green bell pepper, cut into strips
- ½ red bell pepper, cut into strips
- ¼ onion, sliced

Directions:
1. Preheat the air fryer to 200°C.
2. Unfold the chicken breast slices on a clean work surface. Rub with olive oil, then drizzle with lime juice and sprinkle with taco seasoning.
3. Top the chicken slices with equal amount of bell peppers and onion. Roll them up and secure with toothpicks.
4. Arrange the chicken roll-ups in the preheated air fryer. Air fry for 12 minutes or until the internal temperature of the chicken reaches at least 75°C. Flip the chicken roll-ups halfway through.
5. Remove the chicken from the air fryer. Discard the toothpicks and serve immediately.

Cajun Chicken With Vegetables

Servings: 6
Cooking Time: 20 Minutes

Ingredients:
- 450g chicken breast, boneless & diced
- 1 tbsp Cajun seasoning
- 400g grape tomatoes
- ⅛ tsp dried thyme
- ⅛ tsp dried oregano
- 1 tsp smoked paprika
- 1 zucchini, diced
- 30ml olive oil
- 1 bell pepper, diced
- 1 tsp onion powder
- 1 ½ tsp garlic powder
- Pepper
- Salt

Directions:
1. In a bowl, toss chicken with vegetables, oil, herb, spices, and salt until well coated.
2. Insert a crisper plate in the Ninja Foodi air fryer baskets.
3. Add chicken and vegetable mixture to both baskets.
4. Select zone 1, then select "air fry" mode and set the temperature to 390 degrees F for 20 minutes. Press "match" to match zone 2 settings to zone 1. Press "start/stop" to begin.

Nutrition:
- (Per serving) Calories 153 | Fat 6.9g | Sodium 98mg | Carbs 6g | Fiber 1.6g | Sugar 3.5g | Protein 17.4g

Marinated Chicken Legs

Servings: 6
Cooking Time: 28 Minutes

Ingredients:
- 6 chicken legs
- 15ml olive oil
- 1 tsp ground mustard
- 36g brown sugar
- ¼ tsp cayenne
- 1 tsp smoked paprika
- 1 tsp garlic powder
- 1 tsp onion powder
- Pepper
- Salt

Directions:
1. Add the chicken legs and the remaining ingredients into a zip-lock bag. Seal the bag and place in the refrigerator for 4 hours.
2. Insert a crisper plate in the Ninja Foodi air fryer baskets.
3. Place the marinated chicken legs in both baskets.
4. Select zone 1, then select "bake" mode and set the temperature to 390 degrees F for 25-28 minutes. Press "match" to match zone 2 settings to zone 1. Press "start/stop" to begin.

Nutrition:
- (Per serving) Calories 308 | Fat 17.9g | Sodium 128mg | Carbs 5.5g | Fiber 0.3g | Sugar 4.7g | Protein 29.9g

Air-fried Turkey Breast With Roasted Green Bean Casserole

Servings: 4
Cooking Time: 50 Minutes
Ingredients:
- FOR THE TURKEY BREAST
- 2 teaspoons unsalted butter, at room temperature
- 1 bone-in split turkey breast (3 pounds), thawed if frozen
- 1 teaspoon poultry seasoning
- ½ teaspoon kosher salt
- ⅓ teaspoon freshly ground black pepper
- FOR THE GREEN BEAN CASSEROLE
- 1 (10.5-ounce) can condensed cream of mushroom soup
- ½ cup whole milk
- 1 cup store-bought crispy fried onions, divided
- ¼ teaspoon kosher salt
- ¼ teaspoon freshly ground black pepper
- 1 pound green beans, trimmed
- ¼ cup panko bread crumbs
- Nonstick cooking spray

Directions:
1. To prep the turkey breast: Spread the butter over the skin side of the turkey. Season with the poultry seasoning, salt, and black pepper.
2. To prep the green bean casserole: In a medium bowl, combine the soup, milk, ½ cup of crispy onions, the salt, and black pepper.
3. To cook the turkey and beans:
4. Install a crisper plate in the Zone 1 basket. Place the turkey skin-side up in the basket and insert the basket in the unit. Place the green beans in the Zone 2 basket and insert the basket in the unit.
5. Select Zone 1, select AIR FRY, set the temperature to 360°F, and set the time to 50 minutes.
6. Select Zone 2, select ROAST, set the temperature to 350°F, and set the time to 40 minutes. Select SMART FINISH.
7. Press START/PAUSE to begin cooking.
8. When the Zone 2 timer reads 30 minutes, press START/PAUSE. Remove the basket and stir the soup mixture into the beans. Scatter the panko and remaining ½ cup of crispy onions over the top, then spritz with cooking spray. Reinsert the basket and press START/PAUSE to resume cooking.
9. When cooking is complete, the turkey will be cooked through and the green bean casserole will be bubbling and golden brown on top.
10. Let the turkey and casserole rest for at least 15 minutes before serving.
11. Per serving
12. Calories: 577| Total fat: 22g| Saturated fat: 6.5g| Carbohydrates: 24g| Fiber: 3.5g| Protein: 68g| Sodium: 1,165mg

Bruschetta Chicken

Servings: 4
Cooking Time: 20 Minutes
Ingredients:
- Bruschetta Stuffing:
- 1 tomato, diced
- 3 tablespoons balsamic vinegar
- 1 teaspoon Italian seasoning
- 2 tablespoons chopped fresh basil
- 3 garlic cloves, minced
- 2 tablespoons extra-virgin olive oil
- Chicken:
- 4 (115 g) boneless, skinless chicken breasts, cut 4 slits each
- 1 teaspoon Italian seasoning
- Chicken seasoning or rub, to taste
- Cooking spray

Directions:
1. Preheat the air fryer to 190°. Spritz the two air fryer baskets with cooking spray.
2. Combine the ingredients for the bruschetta stuffing in a bowl. Stir to mix well. Set aside.
3. Rub the chicken breasts with Italian seasoning and chicken seasoning on a clean work surface.
4. Arrange the chicken breasts, slits side up, in a single layer in the two air fryer baskets and spritz with cooking spray.
5. Air fry for 7 minutes, then open the air fryer and fill the slits in the chicken with the bruschetta stuffing. Cook for another 3 minutes or until the chicken is well browned.
6. Serve immediately.

Barbecue Chicken Drumsticks With Crispy Kale Chips

Servings: 4
Cooking Time: 20 Minutes
Ingredients:
- FOR THE DRUMSTICKS
- 1 tablespoon chili powder
- 2 teaspoons smoked paprika
- ¼ teaspoon kosher salt
- ¼ teaspoon garlic powder
- ¼ teaspoon freshly ground black pepper
- 2 teaspoons dark brown sugar
- 4 chicken drumsticks
- 1 cup barbecue sauce (your favorite)
- FOR THE KALE CHIPS
- 5 cups kale, stems and midribs removed, if needed
- ½ teaspoon garlic powder
- ½ teaspoon kosher salt
- ¼ teaspoon freshly ground black pepper

Directions:
1. To prep the drumsticks: In a small bowl, combine the chili powder, smoked paprika, salt, garlic powder, black pepper, and brown sugar. Rub the spice mixture all over the chicken.
2. To cook the chicken and kale chips: Install a crisper plate in each of the two baskets. Add the chicken drumsticks to the Zone 1 basket and insert the basket in the unit. Add the kale to the Zone 2 basket, sprinkle the kale with the garlic powder, salt, and black pepper and insert the basket in the unit.
3. Select Zone 1, select BAKE, set the temperature to 390°F, and set the time to 20 minutes.
4. Select Zone 2, select AIR FRY, set the temperature to 300°F, and set the time to 15 minutes. Select SMART FINISH.
5. Press START/PAUSE to begin cooking.
6. When the Zone 1 timer reads 5 minutes, press START/PAUSE. Remove the basket and brush the drumsticks with the barbecue sauce. Reinsert the basket and press START/PAUSE to resume cooking.
7. When cooking is complete, the chicken should be cooked through and the kale chips will be crispy. Serve hot.

Chicken Cordon Bleu

Servings: 4
Cooking Time: 20 Minutes
Ingredients:
- 4 boneless, skinless chicken breast halves (4 ounces each)
- ¼ teaspoon salt
- ¼ teaspoon pepper
- 4 slices deli ham
- 2 slices aged Swiss cheese, halved
- 1 cup panko breadcrumbs
- Cooking spray
- For the sauce:
- 1 tablespoon all-purpose flour
- ½ cup 2% milk
- ¼ cup dry white wine
- 3 tablespoons finely shredded Swiss cheese
- 1/8 teaspoon salt
- Dash pepper

Directions:
1. Season both sides of the chicken breast halves with salt and pepper. You may need to thin the breasts with a mallet.
2. Place 1 slice of ham and half slice of cheese on top of each chicken breast half.
3. Roll the breast up and use toothpicks to secure it.
4. Sprinkle the breadcrumbs on top and spray lightly with the cooking oil.
5. Insert a crisper plate into each drawer. Divide the chicken between each drawer and insert the drawers into the unit.
6. Select zone 1, select AIR FRY, set temperature to 390 degrees F/ 200 degrees C, and set time to 7 minutes. Select MATCH to match zone 2 settings to zone 1. Press the START/STOP button to begin cooking.
7. When the time reaches 5 minutes, press START/STOP to pause the unit. Remove the drawers and flip the chicken. Re-insert the drawers into the unit and press START/STOP to resume cooking.
8. To make the sauce, mix the flour, wine, and milk together in a small pot until smooth. Bring to a boil over high heat, stirring frequently, for 1–2 minutes, or until the sauce has thickened.
9. Reduce the heat to medium. Add the cheese. Cook and stir for 2–3 minutes, or until the cheese has melted and the sauce has thickened and bubbled. Add salt and pepper to taste. Keep the sauce heated at a low temperature until ready to serve.

Nutrition:
- (Per serving) Calories 272 | Fat 8g | Sodium 519mg | Carbs 14g | Fiber 2g | Sugar 1g | Protein 32g

Air Fried Turkey Breast

Servings: 4
Cooking Time: 46 Minutes
Ingredients:
- 2 lbs. turkey breast, on the bone with skin
- ½ tablespoon olive oil
- 1 teaspoon salt
- ¼ tablespoon dry poultry seasoning

Directions:
1. Rub turkey breast with ½ tablespoons of oil.
2. Season both its sides with turkey seasoning and salt, then rub in the brush half tablespoons of oil over the skin of the turkey.
3. Divide the turkey in half and place each half in each of the crisper plate.
4. Return the crisper plate to the Ninja Foodi Dual Zone Air Fryer.
5. Choose the Air Fry mode for Zone 1 and set the temperature to 390 degrees F and the time to 46 minutes
6. Select the "MATCH" button to copy the settings for Zone 2.
7. Initiate cooking by pressing the START/STOP button.
8. Flip the turkey once cooked halfway through, and resume cooking.
9. Slice and serve warm.

Sesame Ginger Chicken

Servings: 4
Cooking Time: 30 Minutes
Ingredients:
- 4 ounces green beans
- 1 tablespoon canola oil
- 1½ pounds boneless, skinless chicken breasts
- ⅓ cup prepared sesame-ginger sauce
- Kosher salt, to taste
- Black pepper, to taste

Directions:
1. Toss the green beans with a teaspoon of salt and pepper in a medium mixing bowl.
2. Place a crisper plate in each drawer. Place the green beans in the zone 1 drawer and insert it into the unit. Place the chicken breasts in the zone 2 drawer and place it inside the unit.
3. Select zone 1, then AIR FRY, and set the temperature to 390 degrees F/ 200 degrees C with a 10-minute timer. Select zone 2, then AIR FRY, and set the temperature to 390 degrees F/ 200 degrees C with an 18-minute timer. Select SYNC. To begin cooking, press the START/STOP button.
4. Press START/STOP to pause the unit when the zone 2 timer reaches 9 minutes. Remove the chicken from the drawer and toss it in the sesame ginger sauce. To resume cooking, re-insert the drawer into the unit and press START/STOP.
5. When cooking is complete, serve the chicken breasts and green beans straight away.

Nutrition:
- (Per serving) Calories 143 | Fat 7g | Sodium 638mg | Carbs 11.6g | Fiber 1.4g | Sugar 8.5g | Protein 11.1g

Desserts Recipes

Baked Brazilian Pineapple

Servings: 4
Cooking Time: 10 Minutes
Ingredients:
- 95 g brown sugar
- 2 teaspoons ground cinnamon
- 1 small pineapple, peeled, cored, and cut into spears
- 3 tablespoons unsalted butter, melted

Directions:
1. In a small bowl, mix the brown sugar and cinnamon until thoroughly combined.
2. Brush the pineapple spears with the melted butter. Sprinkle the cinnamon-sugar over the spears, pressing lightly to ensure it adheres well.
3. Place the spears in the two air fryer drawers in a single layer. Set the air fryer to 204°C and cook for 10 minutes. Halfway through the cooking time, brush the spears with butter.
4. The pineapple spears are done when they are heated through, and the sugar is bubbling. Serve hot.

Homemade Mint Pie And Strawberry Pecan Pie

Servings: 8
Cooking Time: 25 Minutes
Ingredients:
- Homemade Mint Pie:
- 1 tablespoon instant coffee
- 2 tablespoons almond butter, softened
- 2 tablespoons granulated sweetener
- 1 teaspoon dried mint
- 3 eggs, beaten
- 1 teaspoon dried spearmint
- 4 teaspoons coconut flour
- Cooking spray
- Strawberry Pecan Pie:
- 190 g whole shelled pecans
- 1 tablespoon unsalted butter, softened
- 240 ml heavy whipping cream
- 12 medium fresh strawberries, hulled
- 2 tablespoons sour cream

Directions:
1. Make the Homemade Mint Pie:
2. Spray the zone 1 air fryer drawer with cooking spray.
3. Then mix all ingredients in the mixer bowl.
4. When you get a smooth mixture, transfer it in the zone 1 air fryer drawer. Flatten it gently. Cook the pie at 185°C for 25 minutes.
5. Make the Strawberry Pecan Pie:
6. Place pecans and butter into a food processor and pulse ten times until a dough forms. Press dough into the bottom of an ungreased round nonstick baking dish.
7. Place dish into the zone 2 air fryer drawer. Adjust the temperature to 160°C and set the timer for 10 minutes. Crust will be firm and golden when done. Let cool 20 minutes.
8. In a large bowl, whisk cream until fluffy and doubled in size, about 2 minutes.
9. In a separate large bowl, mash strawberries until mostly liquid. Fold strawberries and sour cream into whipped cream.
10. Spoon mixture into cooled crust, cover, and place in refrigerator for at least 30 minutes to set. Serve chilled.

Apple Wedges With Apricots And Coconut Mixed Berry Crisp

Servings: 10
Cooking Time: 20 Minutes
Ingredients:
- Apple Wedges with Apricots:
- 4 large apples, peeled and sliced into 8 wedges
- 2 tablespoons light olive oil
- 95 g dried apricots, chopped
- 1 to 2 tablespoons granulated sugar
- ½ teaspoon ground cinnamon
- Coconut Mixed Berry Crisp:
- 1 tablespoon butter, melted
- 340 g mixed berries
- 65 g granulated sweetener
- 1 teaspoon pure vanilla extract
- ½ teaspoon ground cinnamon
- ¼ teaspoon ground cloves
- ¼ teaspoon grated nutmeg
- 50 g coconut chips, for garnish

Directions:
1. Make the Apple Wedges with Apricots :
2. Preheat the zone 1 air fryer drawer to 180°C.
3. Toss the apple wedges with the olive oil in a mixing bowl until well coated.
4. Place the apple wedges in the zone 1 air fryer drawer and air fry for 12 to 15 minutes.
5. Sprinkle with the dried apricots and air fry for another 3 minutes.
6. Meanwhile, thoroughly combine the sugar and cinnamon in a small bowl.
7. Remove the apple wedges from the drawer to a plate. Serve sprinkled with the sugar mixture.
8. Make the Coconut Mixed Berry Crisp :
9. Preheat the zone 2 air fryer drawer to 164°C. Coat a baking pan with melted butter.
10. Put the remaining ingredients except the coconut chips in the prepared baking pan.
11. Bake in the preheated air fryer for 20 minutes.
12. Serve garnished with the coconut chips.

Bourbon Bread Pudding And Ricotta Lemon Poppy Seed Cake

Servings: 8
Cooking Time: 55 Minutes
Ingredients:
- Bourbon Bread Pudding :
- 3 slices whole grain bread, cubed
- 1 large egg
- 240 ml whole milk
- 2 tablespoons bourbon, or peach juice
- ½ teaspoons vanilla extract
- 4 tablespoons maple syrup, divided
- ½ teaspoons ground cinnamon
- 2 teaspoons sparkling sugar
- Ricotta Lemon Poppy Seed Cake:
- Unsalted butter, at room temperature
- 110 g almond flour
- 100 g granulated sugar
- 3 large eggs
- 55 g heavy cream
- 60 g full-fat ricotta cheese
- 55 g coconut oil, melted
- 2 tablespoons poppy seeds
- 1 teaspoon baking powder
- 1 teaspoon pure lemon extract
- Grated zest and juice of 1 lemon, plus more zest for garnish

Directions:
1. Make the Bourbon Bread Pudding :
2. Preheat the zone 1 air fryer drawer to 135°C.
3. Spray a baking pan with nonstick cooking spray, then place the bread cubes in the pan.
4. In a medium bowl, whisk together the egg, milk, bourbon, vanilla extract, 3 tablespoons of maple syrup, and cinnamon. Pour the egg mixture over the bread and press down with a spatula to coat all the bread, then sprinkle the sparkling sugar on top and bake for 20 minutes in the zone 1 drawer.
5. Remove the pudding from the air fryer and allow to cool in the pan on a wire rack for 10 minutes. Drizzle the remaining 1 tablespoon of maple syrup on top. Slice and serve warm.
6. Make the Ricotta Lemon Poppy Seed Cake :
7. Generously butter a baking pan. Line the bottom of the pan with baking paper cut to fit.
8. In a large bowl, combine the almond flour, sugar, eggs, cream, ricotta, coconut oil, poppy seeds, baking powder, lemon extract, lemon zest, and lemon juice. Beat with a hand mixer on medium speed, until well blended and fluffy.
9. Pour the batter into the prepared pan. Cover the pan tightly with aluminum foil. Set the pan in the zone 2 air fryer drawer. Set the temperature to 164°C and cook for 45 minutes. Remove the foil and cook for 10 to 15 minutes more, until a knife inserted into the center of the cake comes out clean.
10. Let the cake cool in the pan on a wire rack for 10 minutes. Remove the cake from pan and let it cool on the rack for 15 minutes before slicing.
11. Top with additional lemon zest, slice and serve.

Oreo Rolls

Servings: 9
Cooking Time: 10 Minutes
Ingredients:
- 1 crescent sheet roll
- 9 Oreo cookies
- Cinnamon powder, to serve
- Powdered sugar, to serve

Directions:
1. Spread the crescent sheet roll and cut it into 9 equal squares.
2. Place one cookie at the center of each square.
3. Wrap each square around the cookies and press the ends to seal.
4. Place half of the wrapped cookies in each crisper plate.
5. Return the crisper plates to the Ninja Foodi Dual Zone Air Fryer.
6. Select the Bake mode for Zone 1 and set the temperature to 360 degrees F and the time to 4-6 minutes.
7. Select the "MATCH" button to copy the settings for Zone 2.
8. Initiate cooking by pressing the START/STOP button.
9. Check for the doneness of the cookie rolls if they are golden brown, else cook 1-2 minutes more.
10. Garnish the rolls with sugar and cinnamon.
11. Serve.

Strawberry Shortcake

Servings: 8
Cooking Time: 9 Minutes
Ingredients:
- Strawberry topping
- 1-pint strawberries sliced
- ½ cup confectioner's sugar substitute
- Shortcake
- 2 cups Carbquick baking biscuit mix
- ¼ cup butter cold, cubed
- ½ cup confectioner's sugar substitute
- Pinch salt
- ⅔ cup water
- Garnish: sugar free whipped cream

Directions:
1. Mix the shortcake ingredients in a bowl until smooth.
2. Divide the dough into 6 biscuits.
3. Place the biscuits in the air fryer basket 1.
4. Return the air fryer basket 1 to Zone 1 of the Ninja Foodi 2-Basket Air Fryer.
5. Choose the "Air Fry" mode for Zone 1 and set the temperature 400 degrees F and 9 minutes of cooking time.
6. Initiate cooking by pressing the START/PAUSE BUTTON.
7. Mix strawberries with sugar in a saucepan and cook until the mixture thickens.
8. Slice the biscuits in half and add strawberry sauce in between two halves of a biscuit.
9. Serve.

Nutrition:
- (Per serving) Calories 157 | Fat 1.3g |Sodium 27mg | Carbs 1.3g | Fiber 1g | Sugar 2.2g | Protein 8.2g

Savory Almond Butter Cookie Balls

Servings: 10 (1 Ball Per Serving)
Cooking Time: 10 Minutes
Ingredients:
- 1 cup almond butter
- 1 large egg
- 1 teaspoon vanilla extract
- ¼ cup low-carb protein powder
- ¼ cup powdered erythritol
- ¼ cup shredded unsweetened coconut
- ¼ cup low-carb, sugar-free chocolate chips
- ½ teaspoon ground cinnamon

Directions:
1. Stir egg and almond butter in a large bowl. Add in protein powder, erythritol, and vanilla.
2. Fold in cinnamon, coconut, and chocolate chips. Roll up into 1" balls. Put balls into 6" round baking pan and place into the air fryer basket.
3. Set the temperature to 320°F, then set the timer for 10 minutes.
4. Let it cool fully. Keep in an airtight container in the refrigerator up to 4 days and serve.

Cake In The Air Fryer

Servings:2
Cooking Time:30
Ingredients:
- 90 grams all-purpose flour
- Pinch of salt
- 1/2 teaspoon of baking powder
- ½ cup of tutti fruitti mix
- 2 eggs
- 1 teaspoon of vanilla extract
- 10 tablespoons of white sugar

Directions:
1. Take a bowl and add all-purpose flour, salt, and baking powder.
2. Stir it in a large bowl.
3. Whisk two eggs in a separate bowl and add vanilla extract, sugar and blend it with a hand beater.
4. Now combine wet ingredients with the dry ones.
5. Mix it well and pour it between two round pan that fits inside baskets.
6. Place the pans in both the baskets.
7. Now set the zone 1 basket to BAKE function at 310 for 30 minutes.
8. Select MATCH for zone two baskets.
9. Once it's done, serve and enjoy.

Nutrition:
- (Per serving) Calories 711| Fat4.8g| Sodium 143mg | Carbs 161g | Fiber 1.3g | Sugar 105g | Protein 10.2g

Pecan And Cherry Stuffed Apples

Servings: 4
Cooking Time: 20 Minutes
Ingredients:
- 4 apples (about 565 g)
- 40 g chopped pecans
- 50 g dried tart cherries
- 1 tablespoon melted butter
- 3 tablespoons brown sugar
- ¼ teaspoon allspice
- Pinch salt
- Ice cream, for serving

Directions:
1. Cut off top ½ inch from each apple; reserve tops. With a melon baller, core through stem ends without breaking through the bottom.
2. Preheat the air fryer to 175°C. Combine pecans, cherries, butter, brown sugar, allspice, and a pinch of salt. Stuff mixture into the hollow centers of the apples. Cover with apple tops. Put in the air fryer basket, using tongs. Air fry for 20 to 25 minutes, or just until tender.
3. Serve warm with ice cream.

Cream Cheese Shortbread Cookies

Servings: 12 Cookies
Cooking Time: 20 Minutes
Ingredients:
- 60 ml coconut oil, melted
- 55 g cream cheese, softened
- 100 g granulated sweetener
- 1 large egg, whisked
- 190 g blanched finely ground almond flour
- 1 teaspoon almond extract

Directions:
1. Combine all ingredients in a large bowl to form a firm ball.
2. Place dough on a sheet of plastic wrap and roll into a 12-inch-long log shape. Roll log in plastic wrap and place in refrigerator 30 minutes to chill.
3. Remove log from plastic and slice into twelve equal cookies. Cut two sheets of baking paper to fit the two air fryer baskets. Place the cookies on the two ungreased sheet and put into the two air fryer baskets. Adjust the temperature to 160°C and bake for 10 minutes, turning cookies halfway through cooking. They will be lightly golden when done.

4. Let cool 15 minutes before serving to avoid crumbling.

Pumpkin-spice Bread Pudding

Servings: 6
Cooking Time: 35 Minutes
Ingredients:
- Bread Pudding:
- 175 ml heavy whipping cream
- 120 g canned pumpkin
- 80 ml whole milk
- 65 g granulated sugar
- 1 large egg plus 1 yolk
- ½ teaspoon pumpkin pie spice
- ⅛ teaspoon kosher, or coarse sea salt
- 1/3 loaf of day-old baguette or crusty country bread, cubed
- 4 tablespoons unsalted butter, melted
- Sauce:
- 80 ml pure maple syrup
- 1 tablespoon unsalted butter
- 120 ml heavy whipping cream
- ½ teaspoon pure vanilla extract

Directions:
1. For the bread pudding: In a medium bowl, combine the cream, pumpkin, milk, sugar, egg and yolk, pumpkin pie spice, and salt. Whisk until well combined.
2. In a large bowl, toss the bread cubes with the melted butter. Add the pumpkin mixture and gently toss until the ingredients are well combined. 3. Transfer the mixture to a baking pan. Place the pan in the zone 1 air fryer drawer. Set the temperature to 176°C cooking for 35 minutes, or until custard is set in the middle. 4. Meanwhile, for the sauce: In a small saucepan, combine the syrup and butter. Heat over medium heat, stirring, until the butter melts. Stir in the cream and simmer, stirring often, until the sauce has thickened, about 15 minutes. Stir in the vanilla. Remove the pudding from the air fryer. 5. Let the pudding stand for 10 minutes before serving with the warm sauce.

Crispy Pineapple Rings

Servings: 6
Cooking Time: 6 To 8 Minutes

Ingredients:
- 240 ml rice milk
- 85 g plain flour
- 120 ml water
- 25 g unsweetened flaked coconut
- 4 tablespoons granulated sugar
- ½ teaspoon baking soda
- ½ teaspoon baking powder
- ½ teaspoon vanilla essence
- ½ teaspoon ground cinnamon
- ¼ teaspoon ground star anise
- Pinch of kosher, or coarse sea salt
- 1 medium pineapple, peeled and sliced

Directions:
1. Preheat the air fryer to 190°C.
2. In a large bowl, stir together all the ingredients except the pineapple.
3. Dip each pineapple slice into the batter until evenly coated.
4. Arrange the pineapple slices in the zone 1 basket and air fry for 6 to 8 minutes until golden brown.
5. Remove from the basket to a plate and cool for 5 minutes before serving warm

Pumpkin Hand Pies Blueberry Hand Pies

Servings: 4
Cooking Time: 15 Minutes

Ingredients:
- FOR THE PUMPKIN HAND PIES
- ½ cup pumpkin pie filling (from a 15-ounce can)
- ⅓ cup half-and-half
- 1 large egg
- ½ refrigerated pie crust (from a 14.1-ounce package)
- 1 large egg yolk
- 1 tablespoon whole milk
- FOR THE BLUEBERRY HAND PIES
- ¼ cup blueberries
- 2 tablespoons granulated sugar
- 1 tablespoon grated lemon zest (optional)
- ¼ teaspoon cornstarch
- 1 teaspoon fresh lemon juice
- ⅛ teaspoon kosher salt
- ½ refrigerated pie crust (from a 14.1-ounce package)
- 1 large egg yolk
- 1 tablespoon whole milk
- ½ teaspoon turbinado sugar

Directions:
1. To prep the pumpkin hand pies: In a small bowl, mix the pumpkin pie filling, half-and-half, and whole egg until well combined and smooth.
2. Cut the dough in half to form two wedges. Divide the pumpkin pie filling between the wedges. Fold the crust over to completely encase the filling. Using a fork, crimp the edges, forming a tight seal.
3. In a small bowl, whisk together the egg yolk and milk. Brush over the pastry. Carefully cut two small vents in the top of each pie.
4. To prep the blueberry hand pies: In a small bowl, combine the blueberries, granulated sugar, lemon zest (if using), cornstarch, lemon juice, and salt.
5. Cut the dough in half to form two wedges. Divide the blueberry filling between the wedges. Fold the crust over to completely encase the filling. Using a fork, crimp the edges, forming a tight seal.
6. In a small bowl, whisk together the egg yolk and milk. Brush over the pastry. Sprinkle with the turbinado sugar. Carefully cut two small vents in the top of each pie.
7. To cook the hand pies: Install a crisper plate in each of the two baskets. Place the pumpkin hand pies in the Zone 1 basket and insert the basket in the unit. Place the blueberry hand pies in the Zone 2 basket and insert the basket in the unit.
8. Select Zone 1, select AIR FRY, set the temperature to 350°F, and set the timer to 15 minutes. Select MATCH COOK to match Zone 2 settings to Zone 1.
9. Press START/PAUSE to begin cooking.
10. When cooking is complete, the pie crust should be crisp and golden brown and the filling bubbling.
11. Let the hand pies cool for at least 30 minutes before serving.

Nutrition:
- (Per serving) Calories: 588; Total fat: 33g; Saturated fat: 14g; Carbohydrates: 68g; Fiber: 0.5g; Protein: 10g; Sodium: 583mg

Cinnamon-sugar "churros" With Caramel Sauce

Servings: 4
Cooking Time: 10 Minutes

Ingredients:
- FOR THE "CHURROS"
- 1 sheet frozen puff pastry, thawed
- Butter-flavored cooking spray
- 1 tablespoon granulated sugar
- 1 teaspoon ground cinnamon
- FOR THE CARAMEL SAUCE
- ½ cup packed light brown sugar
- 2 tablespoons unsalted butter, cut into small pieces
- ¼ cup heavy (whipping) cream
- 2 teaspoons vanilla extract
- ⅛ teaspoon kosher salt

Directions:
1. To prep the "churros": Cut the puff pastry crosswise into 4 rectangles. Fold each piece in half lengthwise to make a long thin "churro."
2. To prep the caramel sauce: Measure the brown sugar, butter, cream, and vanilla into an ovenproof ramekin or bowl (no need to stir).
3. To cook the "churros" and caramel sauce: Install a crisper plate in the Zone 1 basket. Place the "churros" in the basket and insert the basket in the unit. Place the ramekin in the Zone 2 basket and insert the basket in the unit.
4. Select Zone 1, select AIR FRY, set the temperature to 330°F, and set the timer to 10 minutes.
5. Select Zone 2, select BAKE, set the temperature to 350°F, and set the timer to 10 minutes. Select SMART FINISH.
6. Press START/PAUSE to begin cooking.
7. When the Zone 2 timer reads 5 minutes, press START/PAUSE. Remove the basket and stir the caramel. Reinsert the basket and press START/PAUSE to resume cooking.
8. When cooking is complete, the "churros" will be golden brown and cooked through and the caramel sauce smooth.
9. Spritz each "churro" with cooking spray and sprinkle generously with the granulated sugar and cinnamon.
10. Stir the salt into the caramel sauce. Let cool for 5 to 10 minutes before serving. Note that the caramel will thicken as it cools.

Nutrition:
- (Per serving) Calories: 460; Total fat: 26g; Saturated fat: 14g; Carbohydrates: 60g; Fiber: 1.5g; Protein: 5g; Sodium: 254mg

Pineapple Wontons

Servings: 5
Cooking Time: 15 To 18 Minutes

Ingredients:
- 225 g cream cheese
- 170 g finely chopped fresh pineapple
- 20 wonton wrappers
- Cooking oil spray

Directions:
1. In a small microwave-safe bowl, heat the cream cheese in the microwave on high power for 20 seconds to soften.
2. In a medium bowl, stir together the cream cheese and pineapple until mixed well.
3. Lay out the wonton wrappers on a work surface. A clean table or large cutting board works well.
4. Spoon 1½ teaspoons of the cream cheese mixture onto each wrapper. Be careful not to overfill.
5. Fold each wrapper diagonally across to form a triangle. Bring the 2 bottom corners up toward each other. Do not close the wrapper yet. Bring up the 2 open sides and push out any air. Squeeze the open edges together to seal.
6. Preheat the air fryer to 200°C.
7. Place the wontons into the two drawers. Spray the wontons with the cooking oil.
8. Cook wontons for 10 minutes, then remove the drawers, flip each wonton, and spray them with more oil. Reinsert the drawers to resume cooking for 5 to 8 minutes more until the wontons are light golden brown and crisp.
9. When the cooking is complete, cool for 5 minutes before serving.

Butter And Chocolate Chip Cookies

Servings: 8
Cooking Time: 11 Minutes
Ingredients:
- 110 g unsalted butter, at room temperature
- 155 g powdered sweetener
- 60 g chunky peanut butter
- 1 teaspoon vanilla paste
- 1 fine almond flour
- 75 g coconut flour
- 35 g cocoa powder, unsweetened
- 1 ½ teaspoons baking powder
- ¼ teaspoon ground cinnamon
- ¼ teaspoon ginger
- 85 g unsweetened, or dark chocolate chips

Directions:
1. In a mixing dish, beat the butter and sweetener until creamy and uniform. Stir in the peanut butter and vanilla.
2. In another mixing dish, thoroughly combine the flour, cocoa powder, baking powder, cinnamon, and ginger.
3. Add the flour mixture to the peanut butter mixture; mix to combine well. Afterwards, fold in the chocolate chips. Drop by large spoonsful onto two baking paper-lined air fryer drawers. Bake at 185°C for 11 minutes or until golden brown on the top. Bon appétit!

Lemon Raspberry Muffins

Servings: 6
Cooking Time: 15 Minutes
Ingredients:
- 220 g almond flour
- 75 g powdered sweetener
- 1¼ teaspoons baking powder
- ⅓ teaspoon ground allspice
- ⅓ teaspoon ground star anise
- ½ teaspoon grated lemon zest
- ¼ teaspoon salt
- 2 eggs
- 240 ml sour cream
- 120 ml coconut oil
- 60 g raspberries

Directions:
1. Preheat the air fryer to 176°C. Line a muffin pan with 6 paper cases.
2. In a mixing bowl, mix the almond flour, sweetener, baking powder, allspice, star anise, lemon zest, and salt.
3. In another mixing bowl, beat the eggs, sour cream, and coconut oil until well mixed. Add the egg mixture to the flour mixture and stir to combine. Mix in the raspberries.
4. Scrape the batter into the prepared muffin cups, filling each about three-quarters full.
5. Bake for 15 minutes, or until the tops are golden and a toothpick inserted in the middle comes out clean.
6. Allow the muffins to cool for 10 minutes in the muffin pan before removing and serving.

Sweet Potato Donut Holes

Servings: 18 Donut Holes
Cooking Time: 4 To 5 Minutes
Ingredients:
- 125 g plain flour
- 65 g granulated sugar
- ¼ teaspoon baking soda
- 1 teaspoon baking powder
- ⅛ teaspoon salt
- 125 g cooked & mashed purple sweet potatoes
- 1 egg, beaten
- 2 tablespoons butter, melted
- 1 teaspoon pure vanilla extract
- Coconut, or avocado oil for misting or cooking spray

Directions:
1. Preheat the air fryer to 200°C.
2. In a large bowl, stir together the flour, sugar, baking soda, baking powder, and salt.
3. In a separate bowl, combine the potatoes, egg, butter, and vanilla and mix well.
4. Add potato mixture to dry ingredients and stir into a soft dough.
5. Shape dough into 1½-inch balls. Mist lightly with oil or cooking spray.
6. Place the donut holes in the two air fryer baskets, leaving a little space in between. Cook for 4 to 5 minutes, until done in center and lightly browned outside.

Banana Spring Rolls With Hot Fudge Dip

Servings: 4
Cooking Time: 10 Minutes

Ingredients:
- FOR THE BANANA SPRING ROLLS
- 1 large banana
- 4 egg roll wrappers
- 4 teaspoons light brown sugar
- Nonstick cooking spray
- FOR THE HOT FUDGE DIP
- ¼ cup sweetened condensed milk
- 2 tablespoons semisweet chocolate chips
- 1 tablespoon unsweetened cocoa powder
- 1 tablespoon unsalted butter
- ⅛ teaspoon kosher salt
- ⅛ teaspoon vanilla extract

Directions:

1. To prep the banana spring rolls: Peel the banana and halve it crosswise. Cut each piece in half lengthwise, for a total of 4 pieces.
2. Place one piece of banana diagonally across an egg roll wrapper. Sprinkle with 1 teaspoon of brown sugar. Fold the edges of the egg roll wrapper over the ends of the banana, then roll to enclose the banana inside. Brush the edge of the wrapper with water and press to seal. Spritz with cooking spray. Repeat with the remaining bananas, egg roll wrappers, and brown sugar.
3. To prep the hot fudge dip: In an ovenproof ramekin or bowl, combine the condensed milk, chocolate chips, cocoa powder, butter, salt, and vanilla.
4. To cook the spring rolls and hot fudge dip: Install a crisper plate in each of the two baskets. Place the banana spring rolls seam-side down in the Zone 1 basket and insert the basket in the unit. Place the ramekin in the Zone 2 basket and insert the basket in the unit.
5. Select Zone 1, select AIR FRY, set the temperature to 390°F, and set the timer to 10 minutes.
6. Select Zone 2, select BAKE, set the temperature to 330°F, and set the timer to 8 minutes. Select SMART FINISH.
7. Press START/PAUSE to begin cooking.
8. When the Zone 2 timer reads 3 minutes, press START/PAUSE. Remove the basket and stir the hot fudge until smooth. Reinsert the basket and press START/PAUSE to resume cooking.
9. When cooking is complete, the spring rolls should be crisp.
10. Let the hot fudge cool for 2 to 3 minutes. Serve the banana spring rolls with hot fudge for dipping.

Nutrition:
- (Per serving) Calories: 268; Total fat: 10g; Saturated fat: 4g; Carbohydrates: 42g; Fiber: 2g; Protein: 5g; Sodium: 245mg

Fried Cheesecake Bites

Servings: 16 Bites
Cooking Time: 2 Minutes

Ingredients:
- 225 g cream cheese, softened
- 50 g powdered sweetener, plus 2 tablespoons, divided
- 4 tablespoons heavy cream, divided
- ½ teaspoon vanilla extract
- 50 g almond flour

Directions:

1. In a stand mixer fitted with a paddle attachment, beat the cream cheese, 50 g of the sweetener, 2 tablespoons of the heavy cream, and the vanilla until smooth. Using a small ice-cream scoop, divide the mixture into 16 balls and arrange them on a rimmed baking sheet lined with baking paper. Freeze for 45 minutes until firm.
2. Line the two air fryer drawers with baking paper and preheat the air fryer to 176°C.
3. In a small shallow bowl, combine the almond flour with the remaining 2 tablespoons of sweetener.
4. In another small shallow bowl, place the remaining 2 tablespoons cream.
5. One at a time, dip the frozen cheesecake balls into the cream and then roll in the almond flour mixture, pressing lightly to form an even coating. Arrange the balls in a single layer in the two air fryer drawers, leaving room between them. Air fry for 2 minutes until the coating is lightly browned.

Delicious Apple Fritters

Servings: 10
Cooking Time: 8 Minutes

Ingredients:
- 236g Bisquick
- 2 apples, peel & dice
- 158ml milk
- 30ml butter, melted
- 1 tsp cinnamon
- 24g sugar

Directions:
1. In a bowl, mix Bisquick, cinnamon, and sugar.
2. Add milk and mix until dough forms. Add apple and stir well.
3. Insert a crisper plate in Ninja Foodi air fryer baskets.
4. Make fritters from the mixture and place in both baskets. Brush fritters with melted butter.
5. Select zone 1 then select "air fry" mode and set the temperature to 360 degrees F for 10 minutes. Press "match" to match zone 2 settings to zone 1. Press "start/stop" to begin.

Nutrition:
- (Per serving) Calories 171 | Fat 6.7g | Sodium 352mg | Carbs 25.8g | Fiber 1.7g | Sugar 10.8g | Protein 2.7g

Apple Crumble

Servings: 4
Cooking Time: 30 Minutes

Ingredients:
- 1 can apple pie filling
- 6 tablespoons caster sugar
- 8 tablespoons self-rising flour
- ¼ cup butter, softened
- A pinch of salt

Directions:
1. Take a baking dish.
2. Arrange apple pie filling evenly into the prepared baking dish.
3. Take a large bowl, add all the remaining ingredients. Mix well.
4. Place the mixture evenly all over apple pie filling.
5. Press "Zone 1" and "Zone 2" and then rotate the knob for each zone to select "Bake".
6. Set the temperature to 320 degrees F/ 160 degrees C for both zones and then set the time for 5 minutes to preheat.
7. After preheating, arrange the baking dish into the basket of each zone.
8. Slide each basket into Air Fryer and set the time for 25 minutes.
9. After cooking time is completed, remove the baking dish from Air Fryer.
10. Set aside to cool.
11. Serve and enjoy!

Chocó Lava Cake

Servings: 4
Cooking Time: 10 Minutes

Ingredients:
- 3 eggs
- 3 egg yolks
- 70g dark chocolate, chopped
- 168g cups powdered sugar
- 96g all-purpose flour
- 1 tsp vanilla
- 113g butter
- ½ tsp salt

Directions:
1. Add chocolate and butter to a bowl and microwave for 30 seconds. Remove from oven and stir until smooth.
2. Add eggs, egg yolks, sugar, flour, vanilla, and salt into the melted chocolate and stir until well combined.
3. Pour batter into the four greased ramekins.
4. Insert a crisper plate in Ninja Foodi air fryer baskets.
5. Place ramekins in both baskets.
6. Select zone 1 then select "air fry" mode and set the temperature to 390 degrees F for 10 minutes. Press "match" to match zone 2 settings to zone 1. Press "start/stop" to begin.

Nutrition:
- (Per serving) Calories 687 | Fat 37.3g | Sodium 527mg | Carbs 78.3g | Fiber 1.5g | Sugar 57.4g | Protein 10.7g

Biscuit Doughnuts

Servings: 8
Cooking Time: 15 Minutes
Ingredients:
- ½ cup white sugar
- 1 teaspoon cinnamon
- ½ cup powdered sugar
- 1 can pre-made biscuit dough
- Coconut oil
- Melted butter to brush biscuits

Directions:
1. Place all the biscuits on a cutting board and cut holes in the center of each biscuit using a cookie cutter.
2. Grease the crisper plate with coconut oil.
3. Place the biscuits in the two crisper plates while keeping them 1 inch apart.
4. Return the crisper plates to the Ninja Foodi Dual Zone Air Fryer.
5. Choose the Air Fry mode for Zone 1 and set the temperature to 375 degrees F and the time to 15 minutes.
6. Select the "MATCH" button to copy the settings for Zone 2.
7. Initiate cooking by pressing the START/STOP button.
8. Brush all the donuts with melted butter and sprinkle cinnamon and sugar on top.
9. Air fry these donuts for one minute more.
10. Enjoy!

Chocolate Muffins

Servings: 12
Cooking Time: 20 Minutes
Ingredients:
- 2 cup all-purpose flour
- 4 tablespoons cocoa powder
- ½ teaspoon baking soda
- 2 teaspoons baking powder
- ½ teaspoon salt
- 1 cup coconut milk
- ½ cup granulated sugar
- 6 tablespoons coconut oil, melted
- 1 teaspoon vanilla extract
- 1 cup dark chocolate chips
- ½ cup pistachios, chopped

Directions:
1. In a bowl, add the flour, cocoa powder, baking powder, baking soda, and salt and mix well.
2. In another bowl, add the coconut milk, sugar, coconut oil and vanilla extract and beat until well combined.
3. Add the flour mixture and mix until just combined.
4. Fold in the chocolate chips and pistachios.
5. Grease 2 silicone muffin tins.
6. Place the mixture into prepared muffin cups about ¾ full.
7. Press "Zone 1" and "Zone 2" and then rotate the knob for each zone to select "Air Fry".
8. Set the temperature to 300 degrees F/ 150 degrees C for both zones and then set the time for 5 minutes to preheat.
9. After preheating, arrange 1 muffin tin into the basket of each zone.
10. Slide each basket into Air Fryer and set the time for 15 minutes.
11. After cooking time is completed, remove the muffin tin from Air Fryer.
12. Place the muffin molds onto a wire rack to cool for about 10 minutes.
13. Carefully invert the muffins onto the wire rack to completely cool before serving.

Soft Pecan Brownies

Servings: 6
Cooking Time: 20 Minutes
Ingredients:
- ½ cup blanched finely ground almond flour
- ½ cup powdered erythritol
- 2 tablespoons unsweetened cocoa powder
- ½ teaspoon baking powder
- ¼ cup unsalted butter, softened
- 1 large egg
- ¼ cup chopped pecans
- ¼ cup low-carb, sugar-free chocolate chips

Directions:
1. Stir erythritol, almond flour, baking powder and cocoa powder in a large bowl. Add in egg and butter, mix well.
2. Fold in chocolate chips and pecans. Pour mixture into 6&quot| round baking pan. Put pan into the air fryer basket.
3. Set the temperature to 300°F, then set the timer for 20 minutes.
4. A toothpick inserted in center will come out clean when completely cooked. Let it rest for 20 minutes to fully cool and firm up. Serve immediately.

Lime Bars

Servings: 12 Bars
Cooking Time: 33 Minutes
Ingredients:
- 140 g blanched finely ground almond flour, divided
- 75 g powdered sweetener, divided
- 4 tablespoons salted butter, melted
- 120 ml fresh lime juice
- 2 large eggs, whisked

Directions:
1. In a medium bowl, mix together 110 g flour, 25 g sweetener, and butter. Press mixture into bottom of an ungreased round nonstick cake pan.
2. Place pan into the zone 1 air fryer drawer. Adjust the temperature to 148ºC and bake for 13 minutes. Crust will be brown and set in the middle when done.
3. Allow to cool in pan 10 minutes.
4. In a medium bowl, combine remaining flour, remaining sweetener, lime juice, and eggs. Pour mixture over cooled crust and return to air fryer for 20 minutes. Top will be browned and firm when done.
5. Let cool completely in pan, about 30 minutes, then chill covered in the refrigerator 1 hour. Serve chilled.

Pecan Brownies And Cinnamon-sugar Almonds

Servings: 10
Cooking Time: 20 Minutes
Ingredients:
- Pecan Brownies:
- 50 g blanched finely ground almond flour
- 55 g powdered sweetener
- 2 tablespoons unsweetened cocoa powder
- ½ teaspoon baking powder
- 55 g unsalted butter, softened
- 1 large egg
- 35 g chopped pecans
- 40 g low-carb, sugar-free chocolate chips
- Cinnamon-Sugar Almonds:
- 150 g whole almonds
- 2 tablespoons salted butter, melted
- 1 tablespoon granulated sugar
- ½ teaspoon ground cinnamon

Directions:
1. Make the Pecan Brownies :
2. In a large bowl, mix almond flour, sweetener, cocoa powder, and baking powder. Stir in butter and egg.
3. Fold in pecans and chocolate chips. Scoop mixture into a round baking pan. Place pan into the zone 1 air fryer basket.
4. Adjust the temperature to 150ºC and bake for 20 minutes.
5. When fully cooked a toothpick inserted in center will come out clean. Allow 20 minutes to fully cool and firm up.
6. Make the Cinnamon-Sugar Almonds :
7. In a medium bowl, combine the almonds, butter, sugar, and cinnamon. Mix well to ensure all the almonds are coated with the spiced butter.
8. Transfer the almonds to the zone 2 air fryer basket and shake so they are in a single layer. Set the air fryer to 150ºC, and cook for 8 minutes, stirring the almonds halfway through the cooking time.
9. Let cool completely before serving.

Baked Apples

Servings: 4
Cooking Time: 20 Minutes
Ingredients:
- 4 granny smith apples, halved and cored
- ¼ cup old-fashioned oats (not the instant kind)
- 1 tablespoon butter, melted
- 2 tablespoon brown sugar
- ½ teaspoon ground cinnamon
- Whipped cream, for topping (optional)

Directions:
1. Insert the crisper plates into the drawers. Lay the cored apple halves in a single layer into each of the drawers . Insert the drawers into the unit.
2. Select zone 1, select AIR FRY, set temperature to 350ºF, and set time to 10 minutes. Select MATCH to match zone 2 settings to zone 1. Press the START/STOP button to begin cooking.
3. Meanwhile, mix the oats, melted butter, brown sugar, and cinnamon to form the topping.
4. Add the topping to the apple halves when they've cooked for 10 minutes.
5. Select zone 1, select BAKE, set temperature to 390ºF, and set time to 22 minutes. Select MATCH to match zone 2 settings to zone 1. Press the START/STOP button to begin cooking.
6. Serve warm and enjoy!

Churros

Servings: 8
Cooking Time: 10 Minutes
Ingredients:
- 1 cup water
- 1/3 cup unsalted butter, cut into cubes
- 2 tablespoons granulated sugar
- 1/4 teaspoon salt
- 1 cup all-purpose flour
- 2 large eggs
- 1 teaspoon vanilla extract
- Cooking oil spray
- For the cinnamon-sugar coating:
- 1/2 cup granulated sugar
- 3/4 teaspoon ground cinnamon

Directions:
1. Add the water, butter, sugar, and salt to a medium pot. Bring to a boil over medium-high heat.
2. Reduce the heat to medium-low and stir in the flour. Cook, stirring constantly with a rubber spatula until the dough is smooth and comes together.
3. Remove the dough from the heat and place it in a mixing bowl. Allow 4 minutes for cooling.
4. In a mixing bowl, beat the eggs and vanilla extract with an electric hand mixer or stand mixer until the dough comes together. The finished product will resemble gluey mashed potatoes. Press the lumps together into a ball with your hands, then transfer to a large piping bag with a large star-shaped tip. Pipe out the churros.
5. Install a crisper plate in both drawers. Place half the churros in the zone 1 drawer and half in zone 2's, then insert the drawers into the unit.
6. Select zone 1, select AIR FRY, set temperature to 390°F, and set time to 12 minutes. Select MATCH to match zone 2 settings to zone 1. Press the START/STOP button to begin cooking.
7. In a shallow bowl, combine the granulated sugar and cinnamon.
8. Immediately transfer the baked churros to the bowl with the sugar mixture and toss to coat.

Gluten-free Spice Cookies

Servings: 4
Cooking Time: 12 Minutes
Ingredients:
- 4 tablespoons unsalted butter, at room temperature
- 2 tablespoons agave nectar
- 1 large egg
- 2 tablespoons water
- 240 g almond flour
- 100 g granulated sugar
- 2 teaspoons ground ginger
- 1 teaspoon ground cinnamon
- 1/2 teaspoon freshly grated nutmeg
- 1 teaspoon baking soda
- 1/4 teaspoon kosher, or coarse sea salt

Directions:
1. Line the bottom of the air fryer basket with baking paper cut to fit.
2. In a large bowl, using a hand mixer, beat together the butter, agave, egg, and water on medium speed until light and fluffy.
3. Add the almond flour, sugar, ginger, cinnamon, nutmeg, baking soda, and salt. Beat on low speed until well combined.
4. Roll the dough into 2-tablespoon balls and arrange them on the baking paper in the basket. Set the air fryer to 165°C, and cook for 12 minutes, or until the tops of cookies are lightly browned.
5. Transfer to a wire rack and let cool completely. Store in an airtight container for up to a week.

Healthy Semolina Pudding

Servings: 4
Cooking Time: 20 Minutes
Ingredients:
- 45g semolina
- 1 tsp vanilla
- 500ml milk
- 115g caster sugar

Directions:
1. Mix semolina and 1/2 cup milk in a bowl. Slowly add the remaining milk, sugar, and vanilla and mix well.
2. Pour the mixture into four greased ramekins.
3. Insert a crisper plate in the Ninja Foodi air fryer baskets.
4. Place ramekins in both baskets.
5. Select zone 1, then select "air fry" mode and set the temperature to 300 degrees F for 20 minutes. Press "match" to match zone 2 settings to zone 1. Press "start/stop" to begin.

Nutrition:
- (Per serving) Calories 209 | Fat 2.7g | Sodium 58mg | Carbs 41.5g | Fiber 0.6g | Sugar 30.6g | Protein 5.8g

Chicken Thighs In Waffles 79
Chicken Thighs With Brussels Sprouts 71
Chicken Wings 84
Chickpea Fritters 44
Chocó Lava Cake 98
Chocolate Muffins 99
Chocolate Mug Cakes 102
Churros 101
Cinnamon Sugar Chickpeas 35
Cinnamon Toast 15
Cinnamon-raisin Bagels Everything Bagels 18
Cinnamon-sugar "churros" With Caramel Sauce 95
Coconut Cream Mackerel 73
Cottage Fries 36
Crab Cakes 35
Cream Cheese Shortbread Cookies 93
Crispy Calamari Rings 33
Crispy Catfish 71
Crispy Dill Chicken Strips 83
Crispy Pineapple Rings 94
Crispy Tortilla Chips 35
Crumbed Chicken Katsu 76
Crusted Tilapia 58

D
Delicious Apple Fritters 98
Delicious Haddock 65
Delicious Potatoes & Carrots 42
Donuts 28

E
Easy Cajun Chicken Drumsticks 85
Easy Chicken Thighs 82
Easy Pancake Doughnuts 25
Easy Sausage Pizza 12
Egg In Bread Hole 20
Egg With Baby Spinach 19

F
Filet Mignon Wrapped In Bacon 47
Fish Sandwich 69
Fish Tacos 59
French Toast Sticks 26
French Toasts 12

Fried Artichoke Hearts 41
Fried Avocado Tacos 37
Fried Cheesecake Bites 97
Fried Halloumi Cheese 28
Fried Tilapia 68

G
Garlic Herbed Baked Potatoes 40
Garlic Parmesan Drumsticks 81
Garlic Potato Wedges In Air Fryer 42
Garlic Shrimp With Pasta Alfredo 69
Garlic-rosemary Brussels Sprouts 37
Garlic-rosemary Pork Loin With Scalloped Potatoes And Cauliflower 55
Glazed Apple Fritters Glazed Peach Fritters 14
Glazed Scallops 72
Glazed Steak Recipe 45
Gluten-free Spice Cookies 101
Goat Cheese And Garlic Crostini & Sweet Bacon Potato Crunchies 29

H
Harissa-rubbed Chicken 80
Healthy Lobster Cakes 62
Healthy Semolina Pudding 101
Herb Lemon Mussels 65
Homemade Mint Pie And Strawberry Pecan Pie 90
Honey Teriyaki Tilapia 72

I
Italian Baked Cod 67
Italian Chicken & Potatoes 85

J
Jerk Tofu With Roasted Cabbage 43

K
Kale Chips 31
Kielbasa Sausage With Pineapple And Kheema Meatloaf 48
Korean Bbq Beef 52

L
Lamb Shank With Mushroom Sauce 52
Lemon Raspberry Muffins 96
Lemon-pepper Chicken Thighs With Buttery Roasted Radishes 79

Lemon-pepper Trout 63
Lemony Pear Chips 33
Lemony Prawns And Courgette 66
Lime Bars 100

M

Marinated Chicken Legs 86
Miso-glazed Shishito Peppers Charred Lemon Shishito Peppers 32
Mixed Air Fry Veggies 37
Mojito Lamb Chops 50
Mozzarella Arancini 29
Mozzarella Balls 33
Mozzarella Stuffed Beef And Pork Meatballs 54
Mushroom Roll-ups 43
Mushroom-and-tomato Stuffed Hash Browns 14

N

Nashville Hot Chicken 76
New York Strip Steak 45

O

Onion Rings 30
Oreo Rolls 91

P

Panko Crusted Calf's Liver Strips 56
Parmesan Mackerel With Coriander And Garlic Butter Prawns Scampi 61
Parmesan Ranch Risotto And Oat And Chia Porridge 23
Parmesan Sausage Egg Muffins 23
Pecan And Cherry Stuffed Apples 93
Pecan Brownies And Cinnamon-sugar Almonds 100
Perfect Cinnamon Toast 27
Pigs In A Blanket With Spinach-artichoke Stuffed Mushrooms 53
Pineapple Wontons 95
Pork Chops And Potatoes 55
Pork Chops With Broccoli 49
Pork Chops With Brussels Sprouts 44
Potato Tater Tots 31
Potatoes & Beans 38
Potatoes Lyonnaise 15

Prawn Creole Casserole And Garlic Lemon Scallops 64
Puff Pastry 17
Pumpkin Hand Pies Blueberry Hand Pies 94
Pumpkin-spice Bread Pudding 93

Q

Quick Easy Salmon 68
Quinoa Patties 40

R

Ranch Turkey Tenders With Roasted Vegetable Salad 74
Ravioli 30
Roast Souvlaki-style Pork With Lemon-feta Baby Potatoes 51
Roasted Garlic Chicken Pizza With Cauliflower "wings" 80
Roasted Halibut Steaks With Parsley 70
Roasted Oranges 13

S

Salmon Fritters With Courgette & Cajun And Lemon Pepper Cod 61
Salmon Patties 68
Salmon With Fennel Salad 71
Sausage And Cauliflower Arancini 46
Sausage And Cheese Balls 17
Sausage And Egg Breakfast Burrito 13
Sausage Balls With Cheese 34
Sausage Hash And Baked Eggs 19
Sausage Meatballs 46
Sausage With Eggs 16
Sausage-stuffed Peppers 45
Savory Almond Butter Cookie Balls 92
Savory Salmon Fillets 62
Savory Soufflé 13
Seafood Shrimp Omelet 65
Seasoned Flank Steak 49
Seasoned Tuna Steaks 57
Sesame Ginger Chicken 89
Shrimp Po'boys With Sweet Potato Fries 58
Shrimp With Lemon And Pepper 62
Simple Bagels 21
Simple Strip Steak 49

Snapper With Fruit 67

Soft Pecan Brownies 99

Sole And Cauliflower Fritters And Prawn Bake 72

Spicy Chicken Tenders 31

Spinach Omelet And Bacon, Egg, And Cheese Roll Ups 25

Steak And Asparagus Bundles 53

Steak Bites With Cowboy Butter 50

Steak Fajitas With Onions And Peppers 47

Steamed Cod With Garlic And Swiss Chard 60

Strawberry Baked Oats Chocolate Peanut Butter Baked Oats 24

Strawberry Shortcake 92

Stuffed Beef Fillet With Feta Cheese 47

Sumptuous Pizza Tortilla Rolls 50

Sweet And Spicy Carrots With Chicken Thighs 84

Sweet Bites 29

Sweet Potato Donut Holes 96

Sweet Potatoes & Brussels Sprouts 38

Sweet Potatoes Hash 16

Sweet-and-sour Chicken With Pineapple Cauliflower Rice 78

T

Tasty Lamb Patties 54

Tender Juicy Honey Glazed Salmon 67

Thai Chicken With Cucumber And Chili Salad 75

Thai Curry Meatballs 82

Thai Prawn Skewers And Lemon-tarragon Fish En Papillote 63

Tilapia Sandwiches With Tartar Sauce 64

Tomahawk Steak 51

Tuna Patties 66

Tuna-stuffed Quinoa Patties 59

W

Wild Rice And Kale Stuffed Chicken Thighs 77

Wings With Corn On The Cob 78

Y

Yogurt Lamb Chops 56

Z

Zucchini With Stuffing 38